WHO ARE
THE BEST?

A publication of
Leisure Press.
P.O. Box 3, West Point, N.Y. 10996

ISBN 0-88011-256-5

Front cover art: Ted Watts
Cover design: Dee Elling
All text photographs provided by the Public Relations
Department of the professional team of the athlete shown
except for the photo on page 110, used by
permission of Liz Brown.

WHO ARE THE BEST?

THE SPORTS SURVEY BOOK

SECOND EDITION

BOB McMAHON with JAY LEONARD

NEW YORK

DEDICATION

To Robbie and Mark,
my two favorite sports fans.

CONTENTS

Dedication **4**

Preface **6**

1 The Best Sports Cities in America **9**

2 The Allegiance of the Fans **33**

3 The Fans Rate the Players **55**

4 The Players Rate the Fans **87**

5 The All Star Teams of the Decade **98**

6 The 1989 All Stars **114**

7 Childhood Sports Heroes **133**

Acknowledgments **143**

The Author **144**

PREFACE

I have been a sports fan all my life. Like most kids, I got lost at my first game (a Braves-Giants game at the Polo Grounds in 1948). I have also had the thrill of being in the stands for championship games in the four major sports.

I have rooted for the home team since my family moved to Philadelphia in 1949, but many of my favorite teams and heroes were the consistent winners—the big Red Machine of the mid 70's, the unbeatable Celtic dynasty, and the great Colt and Packer teams of the 50's and 60's. Since I attended so many games, I often rooted for any home team on TV because I knew how the thousands of fans in the stands felt.

In 1975 I tried to find out if anyone had ever done a rating of the fans across the country to see who were the best. I called *The Sporting News* to ask them and they hadn't heard of one. I also asked them if anyone had ever rated the cities in this country on performance; again they said no.

I thought here is my chance to do something different. After gathering attendance figures from the various leagues and teams (hockey figures were only available through the teams), I tried many methods before coming up with the "percent of capacity survey." I found by trial and error that taking the maximum number of people that could attend a team's games (capacity) and dividing it by how many actually came, was the most feasible method.

Rating the cities on performance was much easier. After using several methods, I settled on a reverse point system. One point was awarded to the champion in each sport, 2 points to the runner-up, 3 to the best regular season finisher, and 4 to the next best, etc. The city with the lowest average finish would be the best performer for that particular sports year.

I put all the statistics together following the 1975 baseball season and showed them to my brother-in-law, Tom Dean, who is also an avid sports fan. He thought the idea was silly. For the first time I thought I might really have something.

I submitted the statistics to the *Philadelphia Inquirer*, and they declined, but suggested the *Philadelphia Daily News*. The *Daily News* printed the survey and also sent it out on the wire service. I received calls from Buffalo (winner of the attendance survey the first year) and the *Detroit Free Press*, who wanted follow up stories.

I began wondering, "If this is that popular, why don't I call *The Sporting News* and *Sports Illustrated*." I did and they both said no. However, a week later Bob Creamer, Editor of the scorecard section of *Sports Illustrated* called and asked to use parts of my surveys in the magazine. After considerable mind searching and internal debate, I said sure, and in the December 8, 1975 edition of *Sports Illustrated* my surveys appeared. They have been included in the scorecard section many times since then.

After two years of surveying, I wanted to add a human element, to find some way of evaluating the fans in various cities. After gathering opinions from friends, relatives and acquaintances, I decided on four categories: (1) Most enthusiastic (2) Most unfriendly (3) Most knowledgeable and (4) Players favorite cities on the road.

I sent surveys with letters explaining the project to all 97 public relations directors in pro sports and asked for two veterans on each team to answer the questions. Since only 19 returned them, I learned a quick lesson. From there I proceeded to call the public relations directors, who for the most part put me in touch with the players. The first year was rigorous and time consuming, but 172 players responded. Since opinions may not vary significantly from year to year and because of the difficulty in obtaining responses, this survey is done every two years.

The idea for a 1988 All-Star team was developed during the baseball strike of 1981. With no major league baseball to watch, I turned to the minor leagues. I thought it would be interesting to project a starting line-up for every team in baseball. I contacted people in every organization in baseball for their opinions of their own players as well as players from other teams. The 1988 projected line-ups were released in April 1982. However, by the time they appeared, many teams had traded some of their future stars. Rather than include starting line-ups, this book includes the projected 1989 All Stars in each sport based on information gathered from people within the various sports organizations.

When it came time to compose a book based on all the surveys I had completed over the last 9 years, there was one missing ingredient. Enter

Jay Leopold, a 20-year old junior student at the University of Pennsylvania. Jay compiled the mounds of statistics into meaningful form. His first statistical effort produced the City of the Decade. We then both put together our national fans survey and called fans across the country until we had responses from one fan for every area code (105) and one fan for every team in an area (89). Jay's computer expertise and writing skills were invaluable in the completion of this book.

Nine years of surveys, thousands of phone calls and months of compiling and writing have produced a statistical book for sports fans everywhere. We hope you enjoy it.

Bob McMahon

1

THE BEST SPORTS CITIES IN AMERICA

THE EFFECT OF SPORTS TEAMS ON A CITY

The public's perception of a city is important to the well-being of the metropolitan area. If it is perceived as growing and prosperous, more companies will locate there, which will in turn provide more jobs and create an overall better environment. A 1979 report by the Pittsburgh Chamber of Commerce states the economic impact of the Pirates' baseball franchise to be $33 million on the city for that year.

Factors taken into consideration when one forms an opinion of a city might include climate, proximity to resorts or historical monuments, geography, population and the area's natural resources. These are all very important factors that can be seen, felt or measured. However, the element of a city's pride, perhaps the most important factor, is rarely addressed.

Pride can be sparked by a winning tradition in sports. For example, the 1982 World Cup victory did wonders for Italy's citizens—it helped lift spirits burdened by economic and political worries.

In the United States, frenzied parades through the city are traditionally part of sports after winning a championship. Due to the winning traditions of the Bruins, Celtics, and Red Sox, Boston has become one of the best sports towns in the country. Cities with great traditions, such as Boston, are looked upon with great esteem by sports fans across the nation for many reasons: their teams are always in the news (they're never eliminated from the playoffs early in the season), they always seem to attract capacity crowds (a result of their successes), and they seem to have enthusiastic and knowledgeable fans (a result of increased media coverage). Because of a city's popularity across the country, networks, hoping to boost ratings, will frequently broadcast those games nationally, rather than the games involving teams that are not as well liked. Think how often the Red Sox, Yankees, Cowboys, Dodgers and Celtics games are televised each year. This shows the influence that winning teams can have on a city in terms of increased publicity, a positive image, possible increased industrial growth and an abundance of pride leading to a better life for everyone.

However, if a city's sports teams consistently lose, it can lead to trouble. Attendance drops, enthusiasm diminishes, national exposure ceases and general antipathy can descend over a city. What little exposure is received is frequently negative. Ridicule, satirical jokes and scorn all seem to further damage a city's image. For example, after a lengthy streak of losing seasons in the mid 70's, a *Sports Illustrated* article proclaimed Atlanta as "Loserville USA;" far from a prestigious title.

Philadelphia exemplifies the impact that a city with winning teams can have upon its citizens. Led by dreadful teams in the early 70's, Philly was classified as a boring, stagnant city. W.C. Fields' age-old comment "All in all, I'd rather not be in Philadelphia" only made matters worse. Slowly, all four teams improved, climaxing with the 76ers, Flyers, Phillies, and Eagles each reaching the championship finals of their respective sports, beginning in May 1980 with the 76ers. Philadelphia is the only city in history that has achieved this feat. Now, in the early 80's, Philadelphia is described in the news media in very complimentary terms. Winning sports teams do seem to have an invigorating effect on a metropolitan area.

CITY OF THE YEAR

The title "City of the Year" is awarded to the city or metropolitan area whose sports teams compile the lowest average finish. In each sport, the champion and runner-up are assigned first and second place, while the team with the next best regular season record is third, and so on. Upon completion in all four sports, the cities' average finish is calculated, and the "City of the Year" chosen.

Several obstacles were encountered when compiling these statistics. For example, Phoenix has only one team—the Suns—that consistently finishes with a good record. Phoenix cannot, of course, be "City of the Year" based on one team's performance. Therefore, to qualify, a metropolitan area must have teams in three of the four sports surveyed: baseball, basketball, football, and hockey. And what of the teams that were shared by two cities, such as the Golden State Warriors (Oakland

and San Francisco)? In these cases, the two large cities were combined into a single metropolitan area. Other examples include the New York metropolis (with Northern New Jersey), Baltimore-Washington, and in the 80's, Dallas-Arlington. However, this occasionally situated two teams, such as the Colts and Redskins, in the same sport in the same region. To rectify the problem, the numerical finishes of the two teams were averaged. For example, the Colts won the Super Bowl in 1971, while the Redskins checked in at 15th. This gave the Baltimore-Washington metropolitan area eighth place in football. This finish, in turn, was averaged with the finishes in basketball (2) and baseball (12) for a 1971 average of 7.333.

	Baseball	Basketball	Football	Hockey	Average
	2,22	2	1,15	—	
Balt.-Wash.	(12)	(2)	(8)		7.333

Civic pride can be sparked by a winning tradition in sports.

1970

CITY	BASEBALL	BASKETBALL	FOOTBALL	HOCKEY	AVERAGE
1 Minnesota	3	—	2	9	4.666
2 New York	4,11	1	7,14	5	6.000
3 Los Angeles	7	2	6	12	6.750
4 Balt.-Wash.	1,20	4	9,10	—	8.000
5 Detroit	13	12	8	4	9.250
6 Cincinnati	2	9	19	—	10.000
7 Oakland-S.F.	6,9	13	3,18	10	10.250
8 Boston	8	11	22	1	10.500
9 Atlanta	15	5	14	—	11.333
10 Milwaukee	21	3	11	—	11.666
11 St. Louis	16	—	19	2	12.333
12 Pittsburgh	5	—	25	8	12.666
13 Chicago	12,24	7	25	3	13.250
13 Philadelphia	18	6	19	10	13.250
15 San Diego	23	14	11	—	16.000

	BASEBALL	BASKETBALL	FOOTBALL	HOCKEY
CHAMPS	BALT.	N.Y.	K.C.	BOST.
RUNNER-UP	CINCI.	L.A.	MINN.	ST. L.

. . . Minnesota captures 1970 "City of the Year" for the only time of the decade with a 4.666 average.

. . . New York's 6.000 average best finish of the decade—good for second place.

1971

CITY	BASEBALL	BASKETBALL	FOOTBALL	HOCKEY	AVERAGE
1 St. Louis	5	—	10	5	6.666
2 Los Angeles	7	5	7	9	7.000
3 Balt.-Wash.	2,22	2	1,15	—	7.333
4 Detroit	4	8	5	13	7.500
5 New York	10,11	3	9,21	4	8.125
6 Chicago	11,14	4	15	2	8.375
7 Oakland-S.F.	3,5	10	4,8	14	8.500
8 Minnesota	18	—	3	8	9.666
9 Pittsburgh	1	—	19	11	10.333
10 Boston	9	9	29	3	11.750
11 Milwaukee	20	1	15	—	12.000
12 Cincinnati	14	14	12	—	13.333
13 Philadelphia	21	7	22	7	14.250
14 Atlanta	11	13	20	—	14.666
15 Buffalo	—	17	22	9	16.000
16 San Diego	23	14	14	—	17.000
17 Cleveland	24	17	13	—	18.000

CHAMPS	PBGH.	MILW.	BALT.	MONT.
RUNNER-UP	BALI.	BALT.	DAL.	CHIC.

… Baltimore-Washington reaches the finals in three of four sports.
… Baltimore, excluding Washington's Senators and Redskins, compiles an amazing 1.666 average.
… Jumping from 11th, St. Louis logs their only 1st place entry of the decade, despite never having reached the semifinals in any sport.
… Minnesota drops from 1st to 8th.
… The field expands to 17 cities as Buffalo and Cleveland have inauspicious debuts.

1972

CITY	BASEBALL	BASKETBALL	FOOTBALL	HOCKEY	AVERAGE
1 Chicago	3,9	4	11	4	6.250
2 Boston	6	5	14	1	6.500
3 Minnesota	12	—	3	5	6.666
4 Los Angeles	6	1	10	13	7.500
5 Balt.-Wash.	10	9	5,6	—	8.166
6 Oakland-S.F.	1,20	6	7,8	11	8.750
7 Detroit	4	14	11	7	9.000
8 New York	11,15	2	14,24	2	9.000
9 Pittsburgh	6	—	14	9	9.666
10 Houston	5	11	21	—	12.333
11 Cincinnati	2	12	24	—	12.666
12 Atlanta	18	10	11	—	13.000
13 Cleveland	17	15	8	—	13.333
14 Philadelphia	23	12	13	9	14.250
15 Milwaukee	21	3	19	—	14.333
16 St. Louis	15	—	21	8	14.666
17 Buffalo	—	16	26	12	18.000

	BASEBALL	BASKETBALL	FOOTBALL	HOCKEY
CHAMPS	OAK.	L.A.	DALL.	BOST.
RUNNER-UP	CINCI.	N.Y.	MIAMI	N.Y.

...For third year in a row, the Kings prevent Los Angeles from being a city powerhouse.
...New York unable to win a championship despite reaching basketball and hockey finals.
...Chicago finishes first for only time of decade.
...Boston climbs from 10th to 2nd place.

1973

CITY	BASEBALL	BASKETBALL	FOOTBALL	HOCKEY	AVERAGE
1 Balt.-Wash.	4	5	2,17	—	6.166
2 New York	2,13	1	10,13	4,16	7.5000
3 Detroit	9	9	8	6	8.000
4 Oakland-S.F.	1,7	7	4,8	15	8.000
5 Los Angeles	5	2	16	10	8.250
6 Pittsburgh	13	—	3	10	8.666
7 Boston	6	3	23	3	8.750
8 Kansas City	7	11	10	—	9.333
9 Milwaukee	20	4	5	—	9.666
10 Minnesota	11	—	13	7	10.333
11 Chicago	17,18	6	19	2	11.125
12 Atlanta	19	8	13	12	13.000
12 Buffalo	—	15	19	5	13.000
12 Cleveland	21	13	5		13.000
12 St. Louis	11	—	19	9	13.000
16 Houston	10	12	26	—	16.000
17 Philadelphia	21	17	24	7	17.250

	BASEBALL	BASKETBALL	FOOTBALL	HOCKEY
CHAMPS	OAK.	N.Y.	MIAMI	MONT.
RUNNER-UP	N.Y.	L.A.	WASH.	CHIC.

... Defending champion, Chicago drops to 11th.

... Philadelphia's first half-decade problems escalate.

... After three straight "Top 5" appearances, Balt.-Wash. finally wins "City of the Year" crown.

... Oakland-San Francisco has the best finish of decade (9th), but California Seals continue to weaken average.

... 1973 is Detroit's best year.

1974

CITY	BASEBALL	BASKETBALL	FOOTBALL	HOCKEY	AVERAGE
1 Los Angeles	2	6	3	7	4.5000
2 Pittsburgh	6	—	4	11	7.000
3 Balt.-Wash.	4	6	4,21	—	7.500
3 Boston	10	1	17	2	7.500
5 Buffalo	—	9	.9	8	8.666
5 Minnesota	11	2	—	13	8.666
7 Atlanta	6	11	9	9	8.750
8 St. Louis	8	—	20	2	10.000
9 Chicago	12,23	3	23	3	11.625
9 Oakland-S.F.	1,19	8	8,17	16	11.625
11 Milwaukee	18	2	15	—	11.666
12 Detroit	19	4	14	10	11.750
13 Philadelphia	14	17	16	1	12.000
14 New York	5,21	5	21,24	5,15	12.625
15 Kansas City	16	12	11	—	13.000
16 Cleveland	16	15	11	—	14.000
17 Houston	12	13	26	—	17.000
CHAMPS	OAK.	BOST.	MIAMI	PHIL.	
RUNNER-UP	L.A.	MILW.	MINN.	BOST.	

...Los Angeles is the 1974 "City of the Year."
...Detroit's early decade successes abruptly end.
...In one of the worst turnarounds of the decade for any city, New York slumps from 2nd to 14th.
...Buffalo stampedes from 12th to 5th.

Now that "City of the Year" titles have been annually awarded since 1970, it is fitting to acknowledge a more noteworthy accomplishment, "City of the Early 70's." In order to qualify for this award, a metropolitan area must have participated in the "City of the Year" survey in three of the five years during the first half of the decade. Los Angeles won "The City of the Early 70's" with a 6.8 average.

MID DECADE NOTES
FIVE YEAR AVERAGES

THE BEST		THE WORST	
1. Los Angeles	6.800	1. Houston	15.111
2. Balt.-Wash.	7.433	2. Cleveland	14.583
3. Minnesota	7.999	3. Philadelphia	14.200
4. New York	8.650	4. Buffalo	13.916
5. Boston	9.000	5. Atlanta	12.149
6. Detroit	9.100	6. Cincinnati	11.999
7. Oak.S.F.	9.425	7. Milwaukee	11.866
8. Pittsburgh	9.466	8. St. Louis	11.233

Houston had the worst average in the "City of the Year" competition during the first half of the 1970's.

1975

CITY	BASEBALL	BASKETBALL	FOOTBALL	HOCKEY	AVERAGE
1 Pittsburgh	4	—	1	6	3.666
2 Buffalo	—	4	8	2	4.666
3 Boston	2	3	11	5	5.250
4 Los Angeles	7	17	5	4	8.250
5 St. Louis	10	—	5	10	8.333
6 Philadelphia	8	14	11	1	8.500
7 Oakland-S.F.	3,12	1	3,17	16	8.625
8 Balt.-Wash.	5	2	5,25	18	10.000
9 Minnesota	15	—	2	15	10.666
10 New York	9,10	9	15,22	7,7	10.875
11 Kansas City	6	6	19	17	12.000
12 Chicago	16,17	5	22	12	13.875
13 Houston	23	8	11	—	14.000
14 Cleveland	12	9	22	—	14.333
15 Detroit	24	9	11	14	15.500
16 Milwaukee	21	12	17	—	16.666
17 Atlanta	22	16	24	11	18.250

CHAMPS	CINCI.	OAK.	PBGH.	PHIL.
RUNNER-UP	BOST.	WASH.	MINN.	BUFF.

... Baltimore-Washington drops from "Top 5" for 1st time in the decade.
... The 1975 "City of the Year" is Pittsburgh, checking in with a 3.666 average.
... For fourth straight year, Oakland-San Francisco has at least one team reach the championship series.

1976

CITY	BASEBALL	BASKETBALL	FOOTBALL	HOCKEY	AVERAGE
1 Pittsburgh	4	–	1	8	4.333
2 Los Angeles	4	9	3	6	5.500
3 Buffalo	–	6	11	4	7.000
4 Philadelphia	3	6	18	2	7.250
5 Boston	11	1	22	3	9.250
6 Minnesota	10	–	3	16	9.666
7 Balt.-Wash.	7	5	8,11	18	9.875
8 Oakland-S.F.	8,18	3	5,15	14	10.500
9 New York	2,9	11	15,22	5,13	11.000
10 St.Louis	20	–	5	12	12.333
11 Cleveland	12	4	22	–	12.666
12 Kansas City	6	16	15	17	13.500
13 Detroit	17	15	13	15	15.000
14 Chicago	16,22	18	18	8	15.750
15 Houston	13	9	8	–	16.666
15 Milwaukee	21	11	18	–	16.666
17 Atlanta	24	17	18	8	16.750

CHAMPS	CINCI.	BOST.	PBGH.	BUFF.
RUNNER-UP	N.Y.	PHENX.	DALL.	PHIL.

...Pittsburgh wins title for second straight year.
...Buffalo places in "Top 5" for third year in a row.
...Atlanta sets record for futility—two consecutive last place finishes.
...11th place an accomplishment for Cleveland.

1977

CITY	BASEBALL	BASKETBALL	FOOTBALL	HOCKEY	AVERAGE
1 Los Angeles	2	3	3	6	3.500
2 Boston	5	8	4	2	4.750
3 Pittsburgh	7	—	7	7	7.000
4 Philadelphia	4	2	21	3	7.500
5 Balt.-Wash.	5	6	4,7	16	8.125
6 Minnesota	11	—	2	12	8.333
7 St.Louis	12	—	7	10	9.666
8 Denver	—	4	11	17	10.666
9 Oakland-S.F.	15,24	7	1,13	—	11.167
10 Kansas City	3	13	18	—	11.333
11 Chicago	9,13	8	14	13	11.500
12 Houston	13	5	18	—	12.000
13 Detroit	17	8	15	—	14..500
14 New York	1,23	13,22	24,24	4,11	15.250
14 Seattle	22	13	26	—	15.250
16 Cleveland	19	12	11	13	16.750
17 Buffalo	—	20	26	5	17.000
18 Atlanta	25	19	21	9	18.500
19 Milwaukee	21	21	23	—	21.666

	BASEBALL	BASKETBALL	FOOTBALL	HOCKEY
CHAMPS	N.Y.	PORT.	OAK.	MONT.
RUNNER-UP	L.A.	PHIL.	MINN.	BOST.

...Los Angeles continues their decade of dominance with lowest average yet.
...1977 is Boston's finest, good for second place.
...Milwaukee's 21.666 is worst finish for any city in any year
...Expansion and league mergers expand field to 19 cities, as Seattle
and Denver join survey.

1978

CITY	BASEBALL	BASKETBALL	FOOTBALL	HOCKEY	AVERAGE
1 Los Angeles	2	8	4	10	6.000
2 Denver	—	7	2	13	7.000
3 Boston	3	17	7	2	7.250
4 Balt.-Wash.	7	1	4,7	17	7.625
5 Philadelphia	8	4	19	4	8.750
6 Pittsburgh	10	—	7	12	9.666
7 Chicago	15,19	14	7	8	11.500
8 Milwaukee	4	9	23	—	12.000
8 Oakland-S.F.	9,21	10	3,19	—	12.000
10 Atlanta	21	13	14	7	13.750
10 Detroit	13	16	17	9	13.750
12 New York	1,24	10,22	19,24	3,11	14.250
13 Minnesota	18	—	7	18	14.333
14 Cleveland	20	10	17	14	15.250
15 Seattle	26	2	19	—	15.666
16 Buffalo	—	21	24	4	16.333
16 Houston	17	20	12	—	16.333
18 Kansas City	6	18	27	—	17.000
18 St. Louis	21	—	14	16	17.000

CHAMPS	N.Y.	WASH.	DALL.	MONT.	
RUNNER-UP	L.A.	SEAT.	DENV.	BOST.	

. . . St. Louis drops into the cellar after placing 7th.
. . . A ray of hope appears for Milwaukee after the gloom finish of 1977.
. . . Los Angeles takes second straight crown—third in five years.
. . . Boston puts a team in championship series for record 5th consecutive year.

1979

CITY	BASEBALL	BASKETBALL	FOOTBALL	HOCKEY	AVERAGE
1 Pittsburgh	1	—	1	8	3.333
2 Houston	8	6	6	—	6.666
3 Philadelphia	13	6	8	5	8.000
4 Boston	5	21	4	4	8.500
5 Balt.-Wash.	2	2	15,23	13	9.000
6 Los Angeles	18	3	6	10	9.250
7 Denver	—	6	6	17	9.666
8 Milwaukee	4	13	13	—	10.000
9 Seattle	22	1	8	—	10.333
10 Atlanta	23	10	8	6	11.750
11 New York	7,24	16,17	15,21	2,3	13.125
12 Minnesota	15	—	13	12	13.333
13 San Diego	21	12	8	—	13.666
14 Kansas City	12	4	26	—	14.000
15 St. Louis	10	—	21	16	15.666
16 Detroit	11	19	18	15	15.750
17 Chicago	17,19	17	18	11	16.000
18 Cleveland	16	19	15	—	16.666
19 Oakland-S.F.	20,25	13	8,28	—	17.833

	BASEBALL	BASKETBALL	FOOTBALL	HOCKEY
CHAMPS	PBGH.	SEAT.	PBGH.	MONT.
RUNNER-UP	BALT.	WASH.	DALL.	N.Y.

… For the third time in last five years, Pittsburgh wins "City of the Year" award with best average of the decade for any city.

…Amazingly high 6th place finish in 1979 the worst for Los Angeles in the 70's and the only time they failed to make "Top 5."

…For the sixth straight year Boston is in the "Top 5."

…After dismal start, Philadelphia concludes 70's with four consecutive "Top 5" years, previewing future successes in the 80's

…Houston springs from 16th to 2nd with a 6.66 average, their only below 10.000 of the decade.

…Oakland-San Francisco plunges to the bottom from 8th place.

…New York puts at least one team in the finals for the 4th year in a row.

It is time to present three more special titles for deserving accomplishments: "City of the Late 70's," "The Best and The Worst Turnarounds," and "City of the Decade." Requirements for participation in the "Late 70's" survey are the same as those for the "Early 70's."

SECOND-HALF DECADE NOTES
FIVE YEAR AVERAGES

THE BEST		THE WORST	
1. Pittsburgh	5.599	1. Atlanta	15.800
2. Los Angeles	6.500	2. Milwaukee	15.399
3. Boston	7.000	3. Cleveland	15.133
4. Philadelphia	8.000	4. Detroit	14.900
5. Balt.-Wash.	8.925	5. Seattle*	13.749
6. Buffalo	9.110	6. Chicago	13.725

* Due to two expansion teams in late 70's

The next chart compares a cities' two half-decade averages and lists those cities that have improved or worsened dramatically as the decade passed. "The Best Turnarounds" depicts the top 5 cities whose "Late 70's" average was better than their "Early 70's." Philadelphia led this category with an amazing turnaround of 6.2 (from 14.200 to 8.000), with impressive progress made by Pittsburgh and Buffalo.

Conversely, "The Worst Turnarounds" lists cities whose second half decade performance deteriorated. Detroit had the dubious distinction of having the worst turnaround by falling to a 14.900 average from 9.100. Atlanta went from bad to worse as they dropped 3.651 places to 15.8 in the "Late 70's."

TURNAROUNDS FROM FIRST–HALF
TO SECOND–HALF OF DECADE

THE BEST		THE WORST	
1. Philadelphia	+ 6.200	1. Detroit	- 5.800
2. Pittsburgh	+ 3.867	2. New York	- 4.250
3. Buffalo	+ 2.667	3. Atlanta	- 3.651
4. Boston	+ 2.000	4. Chicago	- 3.600
5. Houston	+ 1.978	5. Milwaukee	-3.533

To qualify for the "City of the Decade" title, a metropolitan area must have participated in the "City of the Year" survey in seven of the ten years. And the winner is . . .

CITY OF THE DECADE
TEN YEAR AVERAGES

CITY	AVERAGE
1. Los Angeles	6.650
2. Pittsburgh	7.532
3. Boston	8.000
4. Baltimore-Washington	8.179
5. Minnesota	9.632
6. Oakland-San Francisco	10.725
7. New York	10.775
8. Philadelphia	11.100
9. St. Louis	11.916
10. Chicago	11.925
11. Detroit	12.000
12. Buffalo	12.582
13. Kansas City	12.880
14. Milwaukee	13.632
15. Houston	13.874
16. Atlanta	13.974
17. Cleveland	14.886

CITY OF THE DECADE–LOS ANGELES

Los Angeles' sports teams, a model of consistency during the 1970's, have won the "City of the Decade" with an average finish of 6.65. Los Angeles won the yearly title three times during the decade, finishing in the top five each of the first nine years. An unusual down year for the Dodgers resulted in a sixth place finish in 1979.

Pittsburgh won five championships after a slow start in the decade to finish second. Boston won two championships each in basketball and hockey to finish third.

Personnel from the clubs in the two leading cities had these comments about their winning tradition:

Tom Lasorda, Dodgers Manager: "The reason our organization has done so well is that our outstanding scouting department finds players and turns them over to our minor league department that develops the talent. When our players come up, we refine their talent. We take pride in our front office from Peter O'Malley on down. All those people take pride in what they are doing. Everyone has the same attitude. They want to do everything they can to make the Los Angeles Dodgers the best organization in baseball."

Jerry Buss, owner Los Angeles Lakers and Kings: "The Dodgers have built from a firm base. They are a solid organization. We have done the same thing with the Lakers and are headed in that direction with the Kings."

Chuck Noll, head coach Pittsburgh Steelers: "The atmosphere in Pittsburgh is right for winning. The fans are patient and the teams have a chance to develop. The pressure is not as great here as in other places.

Los Angeles earned ''City of the Decade'' honors for the 1970's.

The next chart chronicles championships in the four major sports for the 1970's. Their listing provides a general index of team performances in the major championships throughout the decade.

CHAMPIONSHIPS OF THE 1970'S

CITY	BASEBALL	BASKETBALL	FOOTBALL	HOCKEY	TOTAL
Montreal				5	5
Oakland	3	1	1		5
Pittsburgh	2		3		5
Boston		2		2	4
New York	2	2			4
Balt.-Wash.	1	1	1		3
Cincinnati	2				2
Dallas			2		2
Miami			2		2
Philadelphia				2	2
Buffalo				1	1
Kansas City			1		1
Los Angeles		1			1
Milwaukee		1			1
Portland		1			1
Seattle		1			1

The Dallas Cowboys won two football championships in the 1970's.

1980

CITY	BASEBALL	BASKETBALL	FOOTBALL	HOCKEY	AVERAGE
1 Philadelphia	1	2	4	2	2.250
2 Los Angeles	6	1	2	12	5.250
3 Houston	5	9	4	—	6.000
4 Boston	10	3	12	5	7.500
5 Pittsburgh	12	—	1	13	8.666
6 Kansas City	2	8	18	—	9.333
7 Atlanta	14	6	16	9	11.250
8 Balt.-Wash.	4	11	7,23	17	11.625
9 New York	3,22	11,17	16,21	1,8	12.375
10 Milwaukee	9	7	23	—	13.000
10 San Diego	20	16	3	—	13.000
12 Minnesota	16	—	18	6	13.333
13 Chicago	21,25	18	7	6	13.500
14 Cleveland	15	14	12	—	13.666
15 Seattle	26	4	12	—	14.000
16 Denver	—	18	7	20	15.000
17 Oakland-S.F.	12,18	20	12,27	—	16.500
18 St. Louis	19	—	23	9	17.000
19 Detroit	10	22	27	18	19.250

	BASEBALL	BASKETBALL	FOOTBALL	HOCKEY
CHAMPS	PHIL.	L.A.	PBGH.	N.Y.
RUNNER-UP	K.C.	PHIL.	L.A.	PHIL.

...Philadelphia places three teams in finals—takes "City of the Year" title with the lowest average since the awards inception.

...Denver drops from 7th to 16th.

...Kansas City jumps from 14th to 6th.

...Pittsburgh drops from 1st to 5th as the Pirates slump.

...Los Angeles bounces back with a second place finish.

1981

CITY	BASEBALL	BASKETBALL	FOOTBALL	HOCKEY	AVERAGE
1 Los Angeles	1	6	5	5	4.250
2 Houston	9	2	5	—	5.333
3 Philadelphia	10	3	2	7	5.500
4 Boston	12	1	10	9	8.000
5 Oakland-S.F.	4,16	14	1,14	—	10.500
6 Milwaukee	6	4	22	—	10.666
6 St. Louis	5	—	24	3	10.666
8 Minnesota	23	—	11	2	12.000
9 Cleveland	15	19	5	—	13.000
9 Dallas	13	23	3	—	13.000
11 Atlanta	19	18	3	—	13.333
12 New York	2,22	8,12	25,25	1,13	13.500
13 Balt.-Wash.	7	13	17,19	17	13.750
14 Chicago	14,25	9	17	10	13.875
15 Kansas City	17	12	14	—	14.333
16 San Diego	24	16	5	—	15.000
17 Pittsburgh	20	—	11	15	15.333
18 Denver	—	15	14	19	16.000
18 Detroit	11	22	11	20	16.000
20 Seattle	21	17	25	—	21.000

	BASEBALL	BASKETBALL	FOOTBALL	HOCKEY
CHAMPS	L.A.	BOST.	OAK.	N.Y.
RUNNER-UP	N.Y.	HOUST.	PHIL.	MINN.

…St. Louis vaults from 18th to 6th.
…Third straight year Houston in the "Top 5."
…Pittsburgh drops from 5th to 17th falling out of "Top Ten" after 10 straight appearances.
…Los Angeles wins 4th "City of the Year" title.
…Oakland-S.F. finishes 5th after a dismal 17th in 1980.

1982

CITY	BASEBALL	BASKETBALL	FOOTBALL	HOCKEY	AVERAGE FINISH
1 Philadelphia	6	2	6	9	5.750
2 Milwaukee	2	4	13	—	6.333
3 Boston	6	3	27	5	10.250
4 St. Louis	1	—	17	14	10.666
5 Denver	—	7	6	21	11.333
5 Kansas City	5	19	10	—	11.330
7 New York	16,23	18,11	5,10	1,8	11.500
8 Oakland-S.F.	10,22	10	1,17	—	11.666
9 Balt.-Wash.	3	7	6,27	21	11.875
10 Atlanta	6	13	17	—	12.000
11 Los Angeles	9	1	22	17	12.250
12 Pittsburgh	13	—	13	12	12.666
13 Detroit	14	7	13	20	13.500
14 San Diego	15	22	6	—	14.333
14 Houston	19	7	17	—	14.333
16 Seattle	20	5	22	—	15.666
16 Dallas	24	20	3	—	15.666
18 Minnesota	26	—	17	6	16.333
19 Chicago	10,21	17	22	14	17.125
20 Cleveland	17	23	25	—	21.666

(Based on regular season records in cities with three or more teams—except for champion and runner-up which receive 1 and 2)

CHAMPS	ST. LOUIS	LOS ANGELES	SAN FRAN.	N.Y.
RUNNER-UP	MILWAUKEE	PHIL.	CINCI.	VANC.

...Boston finishes in top 5 for 9th straight year.
...Denver vaults from 18th to a tie for 5th in last year of eligibility
...Philadelphia leads 1980's with a 4.50 average for first three years.
...New York puts at least one team in finals for 7th consecutive year.
...Cleveland drops from 9th to 20th.
...The Rockies move as the city waits for major league baseball.
...Houston falls from 2nd to 13th.

1983

CITY	BASEBALL	BASKETBALL	FOOTBALL	HOCKEY	AVERAGE
1 Philadelphia	2	1	21	4	7.000
2 Milwaukee	9	6	9	--	8.000
3 Boston	17	3	10	3	8.250
4 *Balt-Wash*	*1*	14	1,28	8	9.375
5 Atlanta	8	13	10	--	10.330
6 New York	5,25	7,12	5,15	1,10,9	11.125
7 Los Angeles	5,22	2	3,25	16	11.375
8 Pittsburgh	11	--	5	20	12.000
9 Dallas	18	15	5	--	12.666
10 San Diego	13	20	5	--	12.666
11 Minnesota	22	--	10	7	13.000
12 Detroit	4	16	15	18	13.250
13 St. Louis	14	--	10	17	13.666
14 Kansas City	14	19	21	--	15.000
15 Seattle	26	8	15	--	16.333
16 Chicago	3,21	19	21	5	17.333
17 Oakland-SF	14,19	17	21	--	18.166
18 Cleveland	22	21	15	--	19.333
19 Houston	10	23	27	--	20.000
CHAMPS	BALT.	PHIL.	WASH.	N.Y.	
RUNNERS-UP	PHIL.	L.A.	MIAMI	EDM.	

. . . Atlanta cracks "Top 5" for first time ever.
. . . Philadelphia wins "City of the Year" again.
. . . The Rockies move as Denver waits for major league baseball.
. . . Dallas leaps from 16th to 9th.
. . . In two short years, Houston plummets from 2nd to cellar.
. . . Devils give New York area three hockey teams.
. . . Anaheim incorporated into the L.A. metropolitan area in the 1983 survey due to Raiders' move to Los Angeles.

Here are best and worst cities of the "Early 80's" as of the end of the 1983 season.

THE 1980's MID- DECADE NOTES FOUR YEAR AVERAGES

THE BEST

1.	Philadelphia	5.125
2.	Los Angeles	8.202
3.	Boston	8.500
4.	Milwaukee	9.500
5.	Houston	11.416
6.	Atlanta	11.730
7.	Balt.-Wash	11.647
8.	New York	12.127
9.	Pittsburgh	12.166
10.	Kansas City	12.500

THE WORST

1.	Cleveland	16.917
2.	Seattle	16.750
3.	Detroit	15.500
4.	Chicago	15.428
5.	Oakland-SF	14.208
6.	Denver	14.111
7.	Dallas	13.777
8.	San Diego	13.750
9.	Minnesota	13.667
10.	St. Louis	13.000

. . . At its current pace, Philadelphia will compile the best "half decade" performance yet.
. . . Pittsburgh drops from its accustomed spot near the top.
. . . Despite erratic peformance, Houston checks in at 5th place.
. . . Denver's poor showing bumps them from "City of the Year" competition.
. . . Cleveland maintains its strong tradition.

The next chart shows the most improvement and worst deterioration of sports cities from the "Late 70's" to the "Early 80's". Milwaukee and Atlanta conducted major turnarounds while Pittsburgh and Denver lost much of their "Late 70's" dominance.

TURN AROUNDS FROM LAST-HALF 1970's TO FIRST-HALF 1980's

THE BEST

1.	Milwaukee	+5.899
2.	Atlanta	+4.070
3.	Philadelphia	+2.875
4.	Houston	+1.784
5.	Kansas City	+1.066

THE WORST

1.	Pittsburgh	-6.557
2.	Denver	-5.001
3.	Seattle	-3.001
4.	Balt-Wash	-2.722
5.	Minnesota	-2.399

TEAMS WITH LONG WINNING STREAKS
Baseball

1) The Boston Red Sox have had winning seasons every year from 1967 through 1982.
2) The Baltimore Orioles have had winning seasons every year since 1968.
3) The Los Angeles Dodgers have had winning seasons every year since 1969.

Football

1) The Raider franchise has had winning records every year from 1965 through 1983, except for 1982.
2) The Dallas Cowboys have had winning seasons every year since 1966.

Hockey

1) The Montreal Canadiens have had winning seasons every year since 1951.
2) The Boston Bruins have had winning seasons every year since 1967.

WINNING CITIES IN THE 1970'S AND 1980'S
1976–77

All four of the Boston and Los Angeles sports franchises had winning records.

1978–79

All four of the Philadelphia sports franchises had winning records.

1979–80

All four of the Boston and Philadelphia sports franchises had winning records.

1980–81

All four of the Boston, Los Angeles, and Philadelphia sports franchises had winning records.

1981-82

Only Philadelphia had all four of its teams with winning records.

1982-83

Philadelphia had 19 consecutive winning teams from 1979-1983. The streak was broken by the 1982-83 Eagles.

2

THE ALLEGIANCE OF THE FANS

The true test of a sports town is the allegiance of its fans. To compare different cities' attendance strictly on total gate numbers is obviously unfair and inaccurate because of population discrepancies and stadium capacity differentials. The most valid way to determine the best fans is to compare average attendances and the average capacities for each city. I have used this method since 1975 (hockey attendance figures were not kept prior to 1975). Other methods have been tried, but are either too complicated or too inaccurate.

To qualify, a city must have at least three teams in the four major sports. Each cities' teams attendance figures for the year are then combined to produce the average percent of capacity (APC) for each city.

Portland, for example, which annually sells out all its Trailblazer games, is not included. This is because all the city's ticket dollars are funnelled into the one sport, thus creating an abnormally high APC.

AVERAGE ATTENDANCE
PERCENTAGE OF CAPACITY
1975

CITY	BASEBALL	BASKETBALL	FOOTBALL	HOCKEY	APC
Buffalo	— —	12,115 70%	78,142 97%	15,858 100%	89.0%
Boston	22,707 65%	13,307 87%	56,072 92%	14,999 99%	85.7%
Milwaukee	16,621 31%	10,611 97%	54,745 99%	— —	75.8%
New York	20,856 38%	18,556 94%	47,629 74%	14,836 91%	74.3%
Los Angeles	31,741 62%	11,545 66%	70,542 77%	14,558 88%	73.2%
St. Louis	21,735 42%	— —	46,078 90%	14,181 79%	70.3%
Philadelphia	25,800 47%	7,237 41%	60,030 91%	17,077 100%	69.8%
Pittsburgh	17,397 33%	— —	46,493 93%	10,971 82%	69.3%
Chicago	12,037 28%	10,704 62%	41,374 74%	15,108 88%	63.0%
Detroit	14,308 28%	7,492 66%	45,327 87%	10,500 65%	61.5%
Minnesota	10,098 21%	— —	47,062 98%	9,590 63%	60.7%
Kansas City	14,958 37%	10,291 62%	59,000 76%	8,510 51%	56.5%
Oakland-S.F.	10,531 21%	8,779 69%	49,711 87%	5,123 41%	54.5%
Balt.-Wash.	14,738 28%	9,360 49%	47,104 83%	9,031 51%	52.8%
Cleveland	14,162 19%	8,161 40%	60,000 75%	— —	44.7%
Houston	10,860 22%	4,572 43%	33,857 68%	— —	44.3%
Atlanta	7,324 15%	5,008 31%	37,857 64%	10,200 65%	44.0%
AVERAGE	33.56%	62.64%	83.82%	75.93%	63.989%

1975—TEAMS WITH THE HIGHEST PERCENT OF CAPACITY

BASEBALL	BASKETBALL	FOOTBALL	HOCKEY
1. Red Sox	1. Bucks	1. Packers	1. Flyers*
2. Dodgers	2. Knicks	2. Vikings	1. Sabres*
			*Tie

... Buffalo's fans take the 1975 APC championship with the highest average in the "Late 70's," 89.0%.

... Fans fill 85.7% of Boston's stadiums (most of the "Late 70's for Boston), good for second place.

... Poor showing by the Braves leads Atlanta to last place with a 44% APC, the worst for any city in the "Late 70's"

... Sixth and fifteenth best performances of "Late 70's" for St. Louis and Cleveland respectively.

Philadelphia Phillies' fans at the Vet. In 1975, the Phillies had a 47% APC in baseball—good for 3rd place in the National League.

AVERAGE ATTENDANCE
PERCENTAGE OF CAPACITY
1976

CITY	BASEBALL	BASKETBALL	FOOTBALL	HOCKEY	AVERAGE
Boston	23,399 66%	13,455 87%	56,709 92%	14,510 96%	85.3%
Buffalo	— —	10,212 58%	72,015 90%	15,858 100%	82.7%
Philadelphia	31,796 56%	12,431 69%	61,234 93%	17,077 100%	79.5%
New York	21,873 40%	16,408 84%	51,424 85.5%	15,858 98%	75.9%
Los Angeles	29,828 53%	12,804 70%	61,395 68%	14,504 89%	70.0%
St. Louis	15,088 30%	— —	45,679 97%	14,621 80%	66.3%
Pittsburgh	13,153 26%	— —	48,756 97%	12,210 75%	66.0%
Detroit	18,808 35%	6,130 55%	72,919 90%	10,236 75%	63.8%
Milwaukee	13,143 25%	10,409 70%	49,907 89%	— —	61.3%
Minnesota	9,171 20%	— —	46,186 95%	9,512 62%	59.0%
Chicago	12,543 31%	6,302 38%	46,266 83%	14,128 83%	58.8%
Oakland-S.F.	9,074 17%	11,971 90%	46,299 81%	5,230 42%	57.5%
Houston	11,217 25%	6,376 57%	45,036 90%	— —	57.3%
Balt.-Wash.	14,306 27%	10,752 57%	50,723 89%	9,512 53%	56.5%
Kansas City	21,541 53%	6,687 41%	60,562 78%	7,310 46%	54.5%
Atlanta	10,765 21%	5,156 35%	40,723 67%	11,250 74%	49.3%
Cleveland	12,321 16%	12,658 63%	55,023 68%	— —	49.0%
AVERAGE	33.81%	62.43%	85.44%	76.64%	64.581%

1976—TEAMS WITH THE HIGHEST PERCENT OF CAPACITY

BASEBALL	BASKETBALL	FOOTBALL	HOCKEY
1. Red Sox	1. Warriors	1. Cardinals*	1. Flyers*
2. Phillies	2. Celtics	1. Steelers*	1. Sabres*
		*Tie	*Tie

…Buffalo's APC drops to 82.7%, good for second place.
…Boston is the 1976 APC champ.
…Cleveland pushes Atlanta out of the cellar, barely.
…New York scores the highest APC of the "Late 70's" (75.9%).

Boston was the APC champ in 1976.

AVERAGE ATTENDANCE
PERCENTAGE OF CAPACITY
1977

CITY	BASEBALL	BASKETBALL	FOOTBALL	HOCKEY	AVERAGE
Boston	28,034 80%	12,619 82%	52,745 86%	13,502 92%	85.0%
Philadelphia	34,178 62%	15,438 84%	56,132 85%	17,077 100%	82.8%
Denver	— —	17,149 98%	62,066 83%	9,817 58%	79.7%
Los Angeles	37,406 66%	12,510 68%	63,141 88%	12,968 71%	73.3%
Seattle	17,612 31%	12,980 92%	60,173 93%	— —	72.0%
New York	21,640 40%	11,331 63%	57,776 84%	16,228 99%	71.5%
Buffalo	— —	7,741 44%	54,990 69%	16,400 100%	71.0%
Chicago	20,795 41%	11,625 70%	50,259 88%	13,167 72%	67.8%
St. Louis	21,003 42%	— —	48,659 95%	13,988 63%	66.7%
Minnesota	15,100 33%	— —	46,535 96%	10,142 66%	65.0%
Oakland-S.F.	12,899 24%	11,691 82%	46,867 88%	— —	64.7%
Pittsburgh	16,950 34%	— —	47,231 94%	11,241 63%	63.7%
Milwaukee	14,866 28%	9,682 65%	54,542 97%	— —	63.3%
Detroit	18,131 34%	7,410 66%	68,399 85%	9,210 68%	63.2%
Houston	14,410 32%	8,486 75%	41,200 82%	— —	63.0%
Balt.-Wash.	15,529 29%	11,408 60%	52,747 92%	11,132 62%	60.8%
Kansas City	24,376 59%	8,061 50%	54,002 69%	— —	59.3%
Cleveland	12,862 18%	13,913 69%	67,422 84%	5,513 30%	50.3%
Atlanta	10,906 22%	5,238 33%	37,646 62%	12,322 80%	49.3%
AVERAGE	39.71%	68.81%	85.26%	73.14%	66.731%

1977—TEAMS WITH THE HIGHEST PERCENT OF CAPACITY

BASEBALL	BASKETBALL	FOOTBALL	HOCKEY
1. Red Sox	1. Nuggets	1. Packers	1. Flyers*
2. Dodgers	2. SuperSonics	2. Vikings	1. Sabres*
			*Tie

…Newcomers Denver and Seattle take third and fifth places in their first year of eligibility.

…Boston takes the APC crown for the second year in a row.

…Buffalo drops to seventh as poor records and severe winter weather hinder the attendance for the Braves and Bills.

…Atlanta is last for the second time in 3 years.

…Cleveland fans fill one-half of their stadiums for the only time in "Late 70's."

…Detroit drops from eighth to fifteenth.

In 1973, the Rams 88% APC in football helped the city of Los Angeles to a 73.3% overall APC rating and fourth place among all cities.

AVERAGE ATTENDANCE
PERCENTAGE OF CAPACITY
1978

CITY	BASEBALL	BASKETBALL	FOOTBALL	HOCKEY	AVERAGE
Philadelphia	33,538 61%	15,718 86%	62,961 95%	17,077 100%	85.5%
Boston	30,138 85%	11,565 75%	58,389 95%	12,368 84%	84.8%
Denver	— —	16,040 92%	74,229 95%	8,898 53%	81.3%
New York	20,992 41%	10,072 66%	64,112 93%	16,239 99%	75.0%
Los Angeles	41,848 73%	13,025 71%	57,463 80%	11,798 81%	71.3%
Chicago	19,978 43%	13,386 81%	56,628 99%	11,088 61%	71.0%
Milwaukee	21,352 43%	10,613 71%	54,574 97%	— —	70.3%
Houston	14,438 32%	9,388 83%	47,625 95%	— —	70.0%
Detroit	22,564 47%	5,448 49%	68,567 86%	13,682 97%	68.5%
Seattle	11,249 20%	12,309 87%	60,815 95%	— —	67.3%
Kansas City	21,194 68%	7,701 48%	56,745 73%	— —	63.0%
St. Louis	16,388 33%	— —	50,844 89%	10,633 57%	63.0%
Pittsburgh	13,772 28%	— —	49,784 99%	10,548 60%	62.3%
Oakland-S.F.	10,687 20%	11,578 79%	44,876 87%	— —	62.0%
Buffalo	— —	6,157 34%	40,916 51%	16,433 100%	61.7%
Balt.-Wash.	14,407 27%	10,891 57%	54,804 95%	10,872 60%	59.8%
Minnesota	10,793 24%	— —	47,622 97%	8,682 57%	59.3%
Atlanta	12,071 24%	7,426 47%	52,434 86%	10,521 69%	56.5%
Cleveland	11,530 17%	11,097 54%	70,845 88%	5,676 31%	47.5%
AVERAGE	40.35%	69.73%	91.33%	69.92%	67.836%

1978—TEAMS WITH THE HIGHEST PERCENT OF CAPACITY

BASEBALL	BASKETBALL	FOOTBALL	HOCKEY
1. Red Sox	1. Nuggets	1. Bears*	1. Flyers
2. Dodgers	2. SuperSonics	1. Steelers*	2. Rangers-Isles
		*Tie	

...Philadelphia's fans are "Number One" in 1978.
...Denver is in "Top 5" for the third straight year.
...Cleveland is last for the second time in three years.
...Chicago has their best year of the "Late 70's."
...Houston rockets from fifteenth to eighth.
...A new stadium helps the Red Wings jump from 68% to capacity to 97%; as a result, Detroit moves up five notches to ninth.

The Pittsburgh Steelers tied for the 1978 APC crown in football.

AVERAGE ATTENDANCE
PERCENTAGE OF CAPACITY
1979

CITY	BASEBALL	BASKETBALL	FOOTBALL	HOCKEY	AVERAGE
Boston	29,786 85%	10,448 68%	58,862 97%	12,976 88%	84.5%
Philadelphia	36,039 66%	12,662 69%	64,635 98%	17,077 100%	83.3%
Milwaukee	25,255 47%	11,098 100%	54,822 97%	— —	81.3%
New York	21,779 40%	9,322 64%	65,678 95%	15,995 98%	74.3%
Denver	— —	15,084 87%	74,261 99%	6,081 36%	74.0%
Houston	24,679 50%	10,886 69%	50,285 100%	— —	73.0%
Detroit	21,746 43%	9,417 84%	64,210 81%	14,691 82%	72.5%
Balt.-Wash.	23,347 73%	13,109 69%	51,950 90%	9,925 55%	71.3%
Los Angeles	35,320 69%	12,065 69%	59,071 82%	9,942 51%	67.8%
Pittsburgh	19,398 37%	— —	49,794 99%	11,506 65%	67.0%
Minnesota	14,274 30%	— —	47,653 97%	10,722 70%	65.7%
Kansas City	28,631 71%	11,059 66%	46,184 59%	— —	65.3%
Oakland-S.F.	11,449 23%	10,681 81%	51,339 90%	— —	64.7%
Chicago	19,618 46%	9,924 53%	56,575 99%	10,392 57%	63.8%
St. Louis	21,133 42%	— —	48,779 95%	9,845 53%	63.3%
San Diego	18,921 39%	9,461 68%	48,643 80%	— —	62.3%
Atlanta	10,280 21%	8,227 52%	57,585 94%	11,495 75%	60.5%
Seattle	10,556 18%	18,225 65%	62,717 98%	— —	60.3%
Cleveland	13,671 27%	8,140 42%	64,980 81%	— —	50.0%
AVERAGE	45.94%	62.13%	91.10%	69.17%	68.835%

1979—THE TEAMS WITH THE HIGHEST PERCENT OF CAPACITY

BASEBALL	BASKETBALL	FOOTBALL	HOCKEY
1. Red Sox	1. Bucks	1. Oilers	1. Flyers
2. Orioles	2. Nuggets	2. Broncos*	2. Rangers-Isles
		2. Steelers*	
		*Tie	

... Boston reclaims the APC crown by finishing first for the third time in four years.
... 1979's 60.5% Atlanta's best in "Late 70's"
... For second straight year, Cleveland last
... Seattle plummets from tenth to eighteenth
... Baltimore-Washington fans leap seven places to eighth
... Chicago drops from sixth to fourteenth
... Cleveland last three out of five years
... Sport by sport APCs for "Late 70's": baseball—37.4755%; basketball—66.5484%; football—87.3326%; hockey—72.2607%; all sports—66.3944

In 1979, Cleveland finished last in the APC overall ratings for the third time in five years.

"Late 70's" Notes

...Boston never finishes below second, wins three out of five years
...Atlanta or Cleveland always last
...Cities whose APC improved every year of "Late 70's": Atlanta, Houston
...Cities whose APC worsened every year of "Late 70's": Boston, Buffalo, Seattle
...Number of Years in the "Top 5": Boston—5; Lost Angeles—4; New York—4; Philadelphia—4; Denver—3; Buffalo—2; Milwaukee—1; St. Louis—1; Seattle—1
..."Late 70's" sports' APCs: baseball—37.47%; basketball—66.55%; football—87.33%; hockey—66.39%.

According to the statistics, the percent of capacity for a sport is inversely proportional to the number of games played. For example, baseball, which has a 162 game schedule, averaged 34.5% of capacity for the years 1975-1979. Football teams during that time played only 14 or 16 game schedules and averaged 87.3% of capacity. Hockey and basketball, which play almost exactly the same number of games, had similar APCs, 72.3% and 66.6% respectively.

"Late 70's" Average Percent of Capacities

	CITY	APC		CITY	APC
1	Boston	85.1%	9	Detroit	65.9%
2	Buffalo	80.9%	9	St. Louis	65.9%
3	Philadelphia	80.2%	11	Pittsburgh	65.7%
4	Denver	78.3%	12	Chicago	64.9%
5	New York	74.2%	13	Minnesota	61.9%
6	Los Angeles	71.1%	14	Houston	61.5%
7	Milwaukee	70.4%	15	Oak-S.F.	60.7%
8	Seattle	66.5%	16	Balt.-Wash.	60.2%
			17	Kansas City	59.7%
			18	Atlanta	51.9%
			19	Cleveland	48.3%

THE MOST SUPPORTIVE FANS—BOSTON

Boston's sports fans were easily the most supportive for the second half of the 1970's. During the five-year period they finished first in APC three times and second twice.

Boston's fans averaged an incredible 85.1% APC for the late 70's, easily beating Buffalo (80.9%) and Philadelphia (80.2%). They consistently averaged between 84% and 86% for the second half of the decade.

General Managers and public relations personnel from the top three finishers made the following observations about their fans:

Harry Sindin, General Manager of the Boston Bruins: "Boston is a natural developmental ground for knowledgeable sports enthusiasts because of the huge educational industry."

Haywood Sullivan, General Manager of the Boston Red Sox: "We are fortunate to have terrific Red Sox fans all over New England who are loyal and knowledgeable. They want a contending team in baseball and we have given them one."

Paul Wieland, Public Relations Director for the Buffalo Sabres: "Buffalo has always been an excellent hockey town. We were an exciting team our first year and have been one since."

Jim Murray, former General Manager of the Philadelphia Eagles: "The Philadelphia fans are the most supportive in all sports. We were selling out when we were a last place team in the early 70's."

Grady Alderman, General Manager of the Denver Broncos: "The Broncos have been sold out every game for the last 13 years (75,103). We also have 15,000 people on the waiting list. The Denver Bears are the only minor league baseball team to draw over 500,000 fans each of the last three years. The fans here are tremendous."

Boston's sports fans were the most supportive during the late 1970's.

AVERAGE ATTENDANCE
PERCENTAGE OF CAPACITY
1980

CITY	BASEBALL	BASKETBALL	FOOTBALL	HOCKEY	AVERAGE
Boston	24,761 74%	14,545 95%	59,165 97%	12,365 84%	87.5%
Milwaukee	24,122 45%	10,901 100%	53,326 96%	— —	80.0%
Philadelphia	33,996 58%	11,700 64%	68,826 97%	17,077 100%	79.8%
Denver	— —	12,859 75%	74,688 99%	9,787 60%	78.0%
Houston	29,208 65%	10,087 64%	49,500 99%	— —	76.0%
New York	24,458 43%	9,341 67%	60,056 88%	15,900 97%	73.8%
Los Angeles	40,115 72%	14,115 81%	52,970 63%	10,444 65%	70.3%
Pittsburgh	22,253 44%	— —	48,991 91%	11,500 72%	69.0%
Minnesota	10,537 23%	— —	45,097 93%	13,094 86%	67.3%
Kansas City	28,609 70%	9,156 55%	56,343 72%	— —	65.7%
St. Louis	17,314 34%	— —	47,096 92%	12,258 68%	64.7%
San Diego	14,603 30%	8,731 63%	50,809 84%	— —	63.0%
Chicago	15,900 39%	8,868 51%	52,135 90%	11,500 67%	61.8%
Detroit	23,491 44%	8,019 36%	65,073 81%	15,400 86%	61.8%
Balt.-Wash.	22,468 42%	11,386 60%	47,304 83%	11,037 61%	61.4%
Atlanta	13,616 26%	10,972 70%	50,957 84%	— —	60.0%
Oakland-S.F.	11,946 22%	8,402 63%	50,181 87%	— —	57.3%
Seattle	10,453 18%	21,725 54%	60,985 94%	— —	55.3%
Cleveland	14,359 19%	7,873 35%	74,227 92%	— —	49.0%
AVERAGE	42.66%	64.56%	84.10%	76.90%	64.08%

1980—THE TEAMS WITH THE HIGHEST PERCENT OF CAPACITY

BASEBALL	BASKETBALL	FOOTBALL	HOCKEY
1. Red Sox	1. Bucks	1. Broncos	1. Flyers
2. Dodgers	2. Celtics	2. Oilers	2. Rangers-Isles

…Boston's 87.5% is the best since Buffalo's 89.0% in 1975.
…Detroit falls from 7th place to a tie for 13th.

In 1980, the Los Angeles Lakers averaged over 14,000 fans per home basketball game.

AVERAGE ATTENDANCE
PERCENT OF CAPACITY
1981

CITY	BASEBALL	BASKETBALL	FOOTBALL	HOCKEY	AVERAGE
Boston	20,393 61%	14,523 95%	57,285 93%	11,147 76%	81.3%
Philadelphia	30,349 52%	11,448 63%	69,666 98%	17,077 100%	78.3%
Milwaukee	18,301 34%	10,936 100%	54,440 97%	— —	77.0%
Los Angeles	34,609 69%	13,119 75%	62,550 91%	11,218 70%	76.3%
New York	23,308 41%	10,651 76%	59,369 87%	16,057 99%	75.8%
Houston	26,426 59%	9,399 60%	50,019 100%	— —	73.0%
Denver	— —	10,325 60%	74,135 99%	8,888 54%	71.0%
St. Louis	19,061 38%	— —	46,697 91%	14,605 81%	70.0%
Minnesota	7,951 17%	— —	45,912 95%	14,175 93%	68.3%
Chicago	15,213 36%	9,505 55%	58,122 100%	12,089 70%	65.3%
Oakland-S.F.	19,107 37%	10.-93 76%	46,792 81%	— —	64.7%
Pittsburgh	11,423 23%	— —	52,013 98%	10,336 64%	61.7%
Kansas City	27,221 67%	8,209 49%	51,311 66%	— —	60.7%
Dallas-Arlington	15,742 38%	7,789 44%	59,672 92%	— —	58.0%
Seattle	11,392 19%	16,465 64%	58,552 91%	— —	58.0%
Detroit	21,280 40%	5,569 25%	77,669 97%	13,325 69%	57.8%
Balt.-Wash.	19,333 37%	9,155 48%	44,529 77%	11,926 66%	57.0%
Atlanta	10,927 21%	8,846 56%	55,307 92%	— —	56.3%
San Diego	10,927 20%	8,846 45%	55,307 97%	— —	54.0%
Cleveland	13,498 18%	5,475 28%	77,460 96%	— —	47.3%
AVERAGE	38.26%	59.94%	91.90%	76.54%	61.74%

1981—THE TEAMS WITH THE HIGHEST PERCENT OF CAPACITY

BASEBALL	BASKETBALL	FOOTBALL	HOCKEY
1. Dodgers	1. Bucks	1. Bears*	1. Flyers
2. Royals	2. Celtics	1. Oilers*	2. Rangers-Isles
		*tie	

...Denver drops out of the top five after 4 straight appearances.
...Boston finishes 1st for the third straight year.
...The averages are down from previous years due to the baseball strike.

In 1981, Houston had a 100% APC in football—good for a
1st place tie with the Chicago Bears.

AVERAGE ATTENDANCE
PERCENTAGE OF CAPACITY
1982

CITY	BASEBALL	BASKETBALL	FOOTBALL	HOCKEY	APC
Los Angeles	90% 45,111	84% 14,755	98% 67,301	69% 11,083	85.3 %
Boston	74% 24,685	99% 15,188	85% 51,968	76% 11,148	83.5 %
Milwaukee	48% 25,370	100% 10,812	98% 54,966		82.0 %
New York	40% 22,409	90% 12,354	98% 66,895	99% 16,058	81.5 %
Philadelphia	49% 30,862	68% 12,362	100% 70,786	100% 17,077	79.3 %
St. Louis	52% 26,399		98% 50,430	81% 14,605	77.0 %
Denver		67% 11,603	100% 74,543	53% 8,702	73.4 %
Houston	44% 19,482	75% 11,710	100% 51,934		73.0 %
Minnesota	22% 11,373		99% 47,687	93% 14,175	71.3 %
Oak-S.F.	36% 18,924	74% 9,796	90% 53,904		66.7 %
Chicago	44% 18,322	52% 9,088	99% 63,395	71% 12,088	66.5 %
Kansas City	71% 28,556	44% 7,438	82% 64,059		65.7 %
Seattle	22% 13,215	72% 18,294	99% 63,827		64.3 %
Pittsburgh	27% 13,475		100% 54,193	64% 10,325	63.7 %
Atlanta	45% 23,102	48% 7,534	98% 59,104		63.7 %
Detroit	42% 21,527	45% 9,910	96% 76,579	70% 13,339	63.3 %
Dallas-Arl.	36% 14,800	54% 9,519	98% 63,544		62.7 %
Balt.-Wash.	42% 21,795	47% 9,020	82% 47,554	66% 11,927	59.3 %
San Diego	38% 20,349	29% 5,477	91% 51,956		52.7 %
Cleveland	19% 13,561	30% 5,769	95% 76,486		48.0 %
AVERAGE	44.26%	63.41%	95.3%	76.54%	69.12 %

1982—THE TEAMS WITH THE HIGHEST PERCENT OF CAPACITY

BASEBALL	BASKETBALL	FOOTBALL	HOCKEY
1. Dodgers	1. Bucks	1. Broncos*	1. Flyers
2. Red Sox	2. Celtics	1. Eagles*	2. North Stars
		1. Oilers*	
		1. Steelers*	
		*Tie	

...Los Angeles finishes 1st as the Dodgers have an unprecedented 90% in baseball.

...Boston is in the top 5 for the 9th straight year.

...Philadelphia becomes the first city to have 100% in two sports.

The Houston Oilers, led by Earl Campbell — the fan's favorite currently playing professional football player — tied for first in APC in football in 1982.

AVERAGE ATTENDANCE
PERCENTAGE OF CAPACITY
1983

CITY	BASEBALL	BASKETBALL	FOOTBALL	HOCKEY	APC
Milwaukee	31,132 59%	10,380 94%	49,226 88%		80.3%
Boston	23,146 69%	15,167 99%	37,263 61%	12,938 88%	79.3%
Philadelphia	28,378 43%	15,775 85%	59,519 82%	16,847 99%	77.3%
Los Angeles	38,318 69%	15,811 90%	50,488 68%	11,535 72%	74.8%
St. Louis	29,667 59%		40,975 80%	12,612 70%	69.7
Minnesota	10,737 19%		57,165 92%	14,481 95%	68.7%
New York	21,927 39%	11,825 59%	57,587 84%	15,008 88%	67.5%
Chicago	22,856 56%	7,343 42%	45,907 70%	17,093 99%	66.8%
Detroit	24,074 46%	12,733 57%	70,496 87%	12,928 67%	64.3%
Dallas	17,480 42%	11,882 67%	53,996 83%		64.0%
Oakland-SF	16,552 31%	8,323 62%	54,967 90%		61.0%
Balt-Wash	26,511 50%	8,990 47%	39,147 69%	12,378 68%	58.5%
Pittsburgh	16,566 30%		52,473 89%	8,407 52%	57.0%
Atlanta	27,532 52%	7,138 45%	43,530 72%		56.3%
San Diego	19,741 38%	4,778 35%	50,062 95%		56.0%
Houston	16,691 37%	7,491 48%	40,069 79%		54.7%
Kansas City	24,859 61%	8,301 50%	30,761 39%		50.0%
Seattle	10,057 17%	14,024 35%	52,178 81%		44.3%
Cleveland	10,680 14%	3,916 30%	80,322 77%		37.0%
AVERAGE	43.73%	58.43%	78.21%	79.80%	65.046%

1983—THE TEAMS WITH THE HIGHEST PERCENT OF CAPACITY

BASEBALL	BASKETBALL	FOOTBALL	HOCKEY
1. Dodgers*	1. Celtics	1. Chargers	1. Black Hawks*
1. Red Sox*	2. Bucks	2. Vikings	1. Flyers*

* Denotes Tie

. . . Milwaukee finally claims APC crown after 5 straight years in "Top 5."

. . . Most cities' APC plummets, due to lengthy football strike. Football attendance significantly hurt.

. . . Seventh place finish for NY worst yet, due to Devils' comparatively poor attendance.

. . . Houston drops to 10th.

. . . Addition of Angels and Raiders to the L.A. metropolitan area in 1983 hurt city's APC.

"EARLY 80's" NOTES

. . . Boston again finishes in first place.

. . . Milwaukee jumps from 7th in "Late 70's" to 2nd in "Early 80's."

. . . Number of years in "Top 5" in "Early 80's": Boston - 4; Milwaukee - 4; Philadelphia - 4; Los Angeles - 3; New York - 2; Denver - 1; Houston - 1; St. Louis - 1.

. . . Most consecutive years in "Top 5": Boston - 9; Philadlephia - 8; Milwaukee - 5; Los Angeles - 3.

. . . "Early 80's" sports APCs: baseball - 42.22%; basketball - 61.58%; football - 87.38%; hockey - 77.44%. This shows gains in baseball and hockey since the "Late 70's," but losses in both basketball and football.

"EARLY 80's" AVERAGE PERCENT OF CAPACITIES

1. Boston	82.9%	11. Pittsburgh	62.9%
2. Milwaukee	79.8%	12. Oakland-SF	62.4%
3. Philadelphia	78.7%	13. Detroit	61.8%
4. Los Angeles	75.9%	14. Dallas	61.6%
5. New York	74.7%	15. Kansas City	60.5%
6. Denver	74.1%	16. Atlanta	59.1%
7. St. Louis	70.4%	17. Balt-Wash	59.0%
8. Houston	69.2%	18. San Diego	56.4%
9. Minnesota	68.9%	19. Seattle	55.5%
10. Chicago	65.1%	20. Cleveland	45.3%

TURNAROUND FROM SECOND-HALF 1970's TO FIRST-HALF 1980's

THE BEST		THE WORST	
1. Milwaukee	+ 9.4%	1. Seattle	- 10.0%
2. Houston	+ 7.7%	2. Los Angeles	- 4.8%
3. Atlanta	+ 7.2%	3. Denver	- 4.2%
4. Minnesota	+ 7.0%	4. Detroit	- 4.1%
5. St. Louis	+ 4.5%	5. Boston	- 2.2%

By an overwhelming margin, football was voted the favorite spectator sport by the fans.

3

THE FANS RATE THE PLAYERS

The Hall of Fame in each sport elects players who were the "best." Most major sports publications choose annual all star teams. However, fans, with the exception of baseball and basketball all star voting, are never asked to choose their favorite players. This survey gave fans the opportunity to choose their favorite teams and players in the four major sports.

194 sports fans took part in the survey. One person from every area code in the country (105) and one person for every team in a metropolitan area (89) participated. For example, four fans were called in the St. Louis area, three for the sports teams, and one for the 314 area code.

According to a nationwide poll of fans, the favorite spectator sport in America is football. Football, with 425 total points, dominated all four regions of the country. Baseball in second place (273), came closest in the East, losing by only 19 points. Basketball and hockey finished third and fourth respectively, with hockey only seven points behind basketball in the East. Other sports that placed well were golf (did best in the Midwest) with 49, tennis, and track and field.

There were many surprising results. For instance, soccer, the world's favorite sport, accumulated only 16 points, while horse racing, the largest attractor of any spectator sport, garnered only 15.

Name in order your three favorite spectator sports.

SPORT	EAST	SOUTH	MIDWEST	WEST	TOTAL
Football	93	104	130	98	425
Baseball	74	47	86	66	273
Basketball	42	51	55	46	194
Hockey	35	10	27	16	88
Golf	15	7	18	9	49
Tennis	10	10	4	10	34
Track & Field	6	6	8	2	22
Soccer	5	2	4	5	16
Horse Racing	3	7	—	5	15
Boxing	1	4	—	6	11
Auto Racing	3	—	1	5	9
Lacrosse	1	1	1	2	5
Wrestling	—	5	—	—	5
Gymnastics	—	—	2	2	4
Bowling	—	1	1	1	3
Raquetball	—	3	—	—	3
Skiing	—	3	—	—	3
Swimming	1	—	1	—	2
Figure Skating	—	—	1	—	1
Rodeo	—	—	—	1	1
Sailing	1	—	—	—	1

THE NEW YORK YANKEES:
America's Favorite Baseball Team

In this country, all baseball fans are either Yankee lovers or Yankee haters. According to this survey, there are more lovers, because the New York Yankees handily beat the Los Angeles Dodgers to capture the title of America's favorite baseball team. The Yanks had extraordinary showings in all regions of the country, finishing first in the East (tied with Boston), Midwest, and South, and third in the West, where the Dodgers reigned. It is interesting to note that the Yanks accumulated 43 points in the South, and only 42 in the East, their home region.

The great Yankee tradition is one of the main reasons for their popularity. According to Phil Rizzuto, Yankee broadcaster, "It was human nature to root for Joe Louis and the Yankees in the 40's. People have been in awe of any player who put on blue pinstripes for generations."

The Red Sox tied the Yanks in the East and placed second in the South, good for third overall. Fourth belonged to the Phillies, who were hampered by an inability to finish higher than third in any region. The Cubs finished higher that any other team in the Midwest (fifth overall), while the Braves accumulated the most points in the South (tenth overall).

The survey also seemed to settle long standing arguments over favorite teams in a metropolitan area. The Yankees proved to be king in New York, while the Cubs reigned in Chicago. Out west, the A's were the Bay Area favorites.

Name your three favorite baseball teams

TEAM	EAST	SOUTH	MIDWEST	WEST	TOTAL
Yankees	42	43	38	27	150
Dodgers	26	19	31	41	117
Red Sox	42	26	16	11	95
Phillies	38	15	21	11	85
Cubs	4	—	37	18	59
Orioles	27	15	2	8	52
Reds	9	12	21	9	51
Athletics	6	8	6	28	48
Cardinals	2	10	26	9	47
Braves	—	23	4	14	41
Mets	30	3	3	3	39
Pirates	20	4	6	6	36
Angels	2	3	6	22	33
Royals	—	4	17	9	30
Giants	5	3	2	19	29
Tigers	1	5	22	1	29
White Sox	1	—	23	5	29
Astros	4	20	3	1	28
Brewers	1	—	19	1	21
Rangers	—	13	2	4	19
Twins	2	—	12	3	17
Indians	3	1	11	—	15
Mariners	—	—	—	14	14
Padres	—	—	3	8	11
Expos	3	—	3	—	6

The N.Y. Yankees captured the title of America's favorite baseball team. Mickey Mantle is shown here pinch hitting a home run on August 4, 1963 to win a game over Baltimore.

Name in order your three favorite baseball players of all time.

Player	E.	S.	M.	W.	Tot.
B Ruth	19	31	19	29	98
M Mantle	10	30	23	28	91
W Mays	26	8	25	26	85
T Williams	30	11	11	19	71
J DiMaggio	18	13	20	14	65
H Aaron	3	24	26	11	64
S Musial	6	17	14	14	51
R Clemente	21	7	8	7	43
S Koufax	12	4	7	7	30
R Jackson	3	6	14	5	28
L Gehrig	-	7	12	8	27
P Rose	1	9	14	3	27
T Cobb	1	8	6	7	22
Y Berra	3	7	1	2	13
A Kaline	2	-	11	-	13
H Killebrew	2	2	6	3	13
D Snider	4	6	1	1	12
J Bench	-	3	8	1	12
B Gibson	-	1	7	3	11
R Maris	5	1	4	1	11
J Robinson	1	7	2	-	10
W McCovey	1	-	-	8	9
W Spahn	-	4	2	3	9
C Yastrzemski	7	-	2	-	9
R Ashburn	5	-	-	3	8
R Roberts	6	-	-	2	8
B Robinson	3	3	-	2	8
F Robinson	6	-	-	2	8
E Banks	-	-	3	4	7
L Brock	-	-	7	-	7
W Ford	2	3	-	2	7
M Wills	1	-	-	5	6
R Campanella	3	2	-	-	5
N Fox	-	-	2	3	5
M Schmidt	4	-	1	-	5
D Allen	2	-	2	-	4
G Brett	-	-	-	4	4
R Carew	-	-	3	1	4
B Feller	1	-	3	-	4
S Garvey	2	-	-	2	4
M Ott	3	1	-	-	4
J Piersall	4	-	-	-	4
B Richardson	-	1	-	3	4
W Stargell	2	-	2	-	4
M Alvio	-	-	3	-	3
T Agee	3	-	-	-	3
L Boudreau	-	-	3	-	3
R Branca	3	-	-	-	3
J Bouton	-	-	-	3	3
G Bush	-	-	-	3	3
P Cavaretta	-	-	-	3	3
D Concepcion	-	1	2	-	3
M Fidrych	-	-	3	-	3

Player	E.	S.	M.	W.	Tot.
J Foxx	3	-	-	-	3
C Furillo	3	-	-	-	3
F Howard	-	1	-	2	3
D Larson	-	-	-	3	3
C Mack	-	3	-	-	3
G Nettles	3	-	-	-	3
N Ryan	-	-	-	3	3
A Simmons	3	-	-	-	3
R Staub	1	2	-	-	3
B Tolan	-	-	3	-	3
P Waner	3	-	-	-	3
B Williams	-	-	3	-	3
J Wynn	3	-	-	-	3
C Boyer	2	-	-	-	2
J Bunning	1	1	-	-	2
J Callison	2	-	-	-	2
S Carlton	-	-	2	-	2
L Clinton	-	-	-	2	2
D Driessen	-	2	-	-	2
R Guidry	-	-	2	-	2
R Hornsby	-	-	-	2	2
C Hubbell	-	-	-	2	2
C Jones	2	-	-	-	2
T McGraw	-	-	2	-	2
E Mathews	-	2	-	-	2
J Morgan	-	1	1	-	2
T Oliva	-	-	2	-	2
A Rodriguez	-	-	2	-	2
J Rudi	-	-	-	2	2
B Schantz	2	-	-	-	2
R Sievers	-	-	2	-	2
R Smith	-	-	-	2	2
E Battey	-	-	1	-	1
K Boyer	-	-	1	-	1
G Brown	-	-	1	-	1
O Cepeda	-	-	-	1	1
R Cey	-	1	-	-	1
R Colavito	1	-	-	-	1
T Conigliaro	1	-	-	-	1
F Crosetti	-	1	-	-	1
A Dark	-	-	-	1	1
D Ennis	1	-	-	-	1
B Goodman	-	-	-	1	1
R Gossage	-	1	-	-	1
G Hodges	1	-	-	-	1
S McDowell	-	-	1	-	1
T Munson	1	-	-	-	1
G Perry	-	-	-	1	1
B Powell	-	-	1	-	1
H Reese	-	1	-	-	1
A Rosen	-	-	1	-	1
E Slaughter	-	-	-	1	1
R Stennent	1	-	-	-	1

BABE RUTH
America's Favorite All Time Baseball Player

"No one ever did more for the game than Babe Ruth. He literally saved the game after the infamous Black Sox Scandal," says Phil Rizzuto, who started his Yankee career in 1941 as a shortstop and has been their broadcaster for the last 26 years.

Babe Ruth, whose name is synonymous with baseball, was voted baseball's most popular player. Mickey Mantle and Willie Mays, who also played in the limelight of New York, finished second and third respectively, with Boston's Ted Williams fourth.

"The Sultan of Swat" began his career as a pitcher with the Red Sox in 1914, winning more than 20 games for them twice. After being traded to the Yankees for financial reasons, he blossomed into one of baseball's greatest hitters and outfielders. He either tied or led the American League in home runs for 12 years. In 22 seasons, Ruth amassed 714 home runs, 2056 walks, a .690 slugging average and for a power hitter, an incredible .342 lifetime batting average.

"He was a great athlete," according to Rizzuto, whose uncle took him to many Yankee games as a youngster. "I was amazed how graceful he was, despite his physique. He was the only person who actually looked good striking out."

In 1935, Yankee scout Birdie Tibbetts, then a rookie, first faced Babe Ruth, in his final year. "He was with the Braves and I was catching in one of my first games. It was a thrill just being behind the plate when he came to bat. Everyone was in awe of him, but we all loved him for what he did."

Some of Babe Ruth's records have been broken, but the stories and legends of baseball's greatest superstar will never be forgotten by fans across the country. He is truly America's all time favorite player.

THE FANS SAY

Blaine Freer—Seattle, Washington: "I grew up with the name of Babe Ruth being synonymous with baseball. There were so many legends and stories. Looking at the boxscores to see what Babe did was part of my upbringing."

Bill Langford—Miami, Florida: "There will never be another ball player like him. He made the game and it wouldn't be the same today without him."

Marty West—Bethesda, Maryland: "Babe epitomized the great baseball player. He had charisma."

Ted Lopatkiewitz—Falls Church, Virginia: "My whole life I've heard of Babe Ruth; he was the Home Run King. In your adult life, you realize what he accomplished. He hit 60 homers when others hit only 12. He symbolizes baseball to me."

Babe Ruth, whose name is synonymous with baseball, was voted baseball's most popular player. Ruth is shown here with Yankee owner Jacob Ruppert on March 8, 1930.

Name your three favorite baseball players currently playing

Player	E.	S.	M.	W.	Tot.
P Rose	25	46	34	29	134
R Jackson	14	17	51	24	106
C Yastrzemski	21	14	16	16	67
M Schmidt	32	8	7	9	56
S Garvey	8	5	17	24	54
G Brett	2	4	16	13	35
R Carew	4	2	12	17	35
J Bench	3	6	12	9	30
F Valenzuela	6	11	3	9	29
R Guidry	12	6	4	2	24
G Nettles	14	-	5	-	19
C Cooper	-	-	18	-	18
S Carlton	8	3	3	2	16
K Hernandez	-	-	12	3	15
F Lynn	8	3	-	4	15
R Henderson	2	-	-	14	16
N Ryan	-	1	2	11	14
D Winfield	6	-	2	5	13
C Fisk	4	5	2	1	12
R Cey	2	4	-	4	10
K Gibson	-	2	8	-	10
B Horner	-	5	-	5	10
B Buckner	-	-	6	3	9
D Concepcion	-	1	6	2	9
R Fingers	?	-	-	7	9
J Rice	-	-	9	-	9
T Seaver	3	4	1	-	8
B Bell	-	7	-	-	7
B Burns	-	-	5	2	7
G Foster	3	-	4	-	7
R Yount	-	-	2	5	7
R Cerone	3	3	-	-	6
T John	3	3	-	-	6
D Kingman	-	2	4	-	6
L Piniella	5	1	-	-	6
G Templeton	-	-	6	-	6
R Gossage	2	2	-	1	5
D Leonard	-	-	-	5	5
T Lollar	-	-	-	5	5
D Parker	2	-	2	1	5
D Evans	2	2	-	-	4
P Garner	-	1	-	3	4
G Hendrick	-	-	4	-	4
G Hubbard	-	2	-	2	4
T McGraw	-	1	3	-	4
R Monday	-	3	-	1	4
R Staub	3	1	-	-	4
G Thomas	-	-	4	-	4
J Bonilla	-	-	1	2	3

Player	E.	S.	M.	W.	Tot.
J Clark	-	-	-	3	3
D Driessen	-	3	-	-	3
B Forsch	-	-	3	-	3
K Hrbek	1	-	2	-	3
C Lansford	3	-	-	-	3
C Lemon	-	-	3	-	3
L Mazilli	3	-	-	-	3
D Murphy	-	3	-	-	3
E Murray	3	-	-	-	3
A Otis	-	-	3	-	3
L Parrish	-	-	3	-	3
J Rudi	-	-	1	2	3
T Simmons	-	-	3	-	3
W Wilson	-	-	-	3	3
C Cedeno	-	2	-	-	2
I DeJesus	-	-	2	-	2
R Dempsey	2	-	-	-	2
G Garber	2	-	-	-	2
P Guerrero	-	2	-	-	2
S Kemp	-	2	-	-	2
B McBride	-	-	2	-	2
J Martin	-	2	-	-	2
J Niekro	-	2	-	-	2
S Sax	-	-	-	2	2
B Sutter	2	-	-	-	2
A Thornton	-	-	2	-	2
A Trammell	-	-	2	-	2
M Trillo	2	-	-	-	2
F White	-	-	2	-	2
M Wilson	2	-	-	-	2
T Armas	-	-	-	1	1
D Baker	-	1	-	-	1
D Baylor	-	-	-	1	1
J Bibby	1	-	-	-	1
L Bowa	1	-	-	-	1
B Dent	-	-	-	1	1
T Foli	1	-	-	-	1
M Keough	1	-	-	-	1
D Lopes	-	-	-	1	1
S McGregor	1	-	-	-	1
B Madlock	-	-	1	-	1
J Mayberry	-	-	1	-	1
O Moreno	1	-	-	-	1
J Morgan	-	1	-	-	1
P Niekro	-	1	-	-	1
T Raines	-	-	-	1	1
W Randolph	-	-	1	-	1
J Sundberg	-	1	-	-	1
D Sutton	1	-	-	-	1
A Wiggins	-	-	-	1	1
J Youngblood	-	-	-	1	1

Mike Schmidt — the Phillies' talented third baseman — finished fourth in the fans' voting for favorite currently active baseball player.

PETE ROSE
"CHARLIE HUSTLE"

"I play hard all the time. I give the fans their money's worth," is Pete Rose's explanation for his popularity in a nationwide poll asking fans to name their favorite currently active baseball player. The only player to approach Rose's popularity was Reggie Jackson, with 106 points to Pete's 134.

Rose has broken some all time records and is on his way to many others. However, none is more important than Ty Cobb's all time record of 4,192 career hits. Pete estimates that he'll break the record in 1985.

Phillies president Bill Giles calls Rose "the hero of the blue collar worker. He does not have the talent that many other players have, but he made himself a great player. He puts out 120% every game."

Broadcaster Rich Ashburn notes, "Rose busts his butt on every play—he's in a class by himself." Steve Rogers, Montreal pitcher, thinks Rose is "the personification of enthusiasm. He is what everyone wanted to be when he played baseball."

Pete added some other reasons for his popularity. "Fans have seen me play for twenty years now. It helps to be in as many All Star games and World Series as I've been in. I've also been in a lot of TV commercials lately, which gives me more national exposure."

Rose's popularity is not confined to the United States, he is also Japan's favorite American player. "I love it over there, and go back almost every year," says Rose.

Fellow twenty year veteran Carl Yastrzemski finished third in the voting followed by Mike Schmidt, Steve Garvey, George Brett, and Rod Carew.

THE FANS SAY

Tim Hagerman—San Francisco, California: "Pete Rose performs well every game, every year."

Joel Colbert—Louisville, Kentucky: "I was an avid Reds fan in the 60's and 70's. Rose was my hero on my favorite team."

Jeff Hudd—Buffalo, New York: "He's enthusiastic. No one enjoys the game more."

James Williams—Little Rock, Arkansas: "I've been reading about Pete Rose for 20 years. I buy six or seven different papers a week, including the *New York Times* and the *Washington Post* to keep up on sports news, and they've run out of words for Pete Rose."

David Turner—Omaha, Nebraska: "I love to watch players who hustle."

THE CELTICS
America's Favorite Basketball Team

The Boston Celtics, one of the most successful teams in professional sports history, was named the most popular NBA team. The Celtics, with supporters nationwide, easily bested their two closest rivals, the 76ers and the Lakers.

"I'm not surprised considering we've won 40% of the league's championships in its 36 year history. We have a great winning tradition," Red Auerbach, Celtic General Manager and former coach remarked. No one is more responsible for the Celtic successes than Red. Three different times he took a losing team and built them into World Champions.

The Celts garnered more points than any team in every region of the country, except the West. There, the Lakers clipped them by two points. The Sixers came in second in the East and South and third elsewhere. All other teams finished far behind the top three.

Other interesting facts:

... Four of the top six teams are from the Atlantic Division.

... Two defunct basketball teams (one from the old ABA) received more votes than the Cleveland Cavaliers

... The Spurs received more votes in the Midwest (7) and West (6) than they did in their home region, the South (5).

Name your three favorite basketball teams

TEAM	EAST	SOUTH	MIDWEST	WEST	TOTAL
Celtics	79	72	65	65	281
76ers	60	50	52	45	207
Lakers	34	32	63	67	196
Knicks	29	6	8	10	53
Bucks	3	—	23	5	31
Bullets	12	12	4	1	29
Supersonics	2	4	8	15	29
Rockets	—	11	6	8	25
Spurs	3	5	7	6	21
Suns	—	4	4	12	20
Nets	14	3	—	2	19
Hawks	1	6	4	5	16
Kings	1	1	10	4	16
Bulls	2	1	10	2	15
Nuggets	—	1	4	10	15
Pistons	2	3	9	—	14
Warriors	3	—	—	11	14
Trail Blazers	3	—	2	8	13
Mavericks	1	9	—	2	12
Clippers	—	—	—	5	5
Pacers	1	—	4	—	5
Utah Stars	—	—	—	4	4
Cinci. Royals	—	—	—	3	3
Cavaliers	—	—	2	—	2

BILL RUSSELL
The Most Popular Basketball Player of All Time

The fans of America chose Bill Russell as their favorite basketball player of all time. "I'm not surprised," said Red Auerbach, Russell's coach and current Celtic General Manager. "He's the greatest player of all time. As for second place Chamberlain, there's no comparison. After all, Bill was named the greatest player of all time in a league poll." The University of San Francisco alum was also voted to the NBA 35 Year Anniversary All Time All Star Team.

Twelve times in his 13 year career, Bill Russell was named to the All Star team. The only year he didn't make it was his rookie season. For his career, Russell averaged an astronomical 22.55 rebounds, 15.1 points, and 42.29 minutes per game to lead the Celtics to 11 World Championships. In his last two seasons (1968,1969), he was a player-coach. More recently, Bill has been a CBS color analyst for CBS' NBA broadcasts.

Russell topped the voting with 169 points, receiving the most points in the West. As for the rest, Chamberlain finished second with 159, and Cousy was third with 115. "I'm happy to see Cousy in the third spot. He was the best guard I've ever seen," noted Auerbach. "I always felt Oscar Robertson was underrated—it's good to see him in sixth place."

THE FANS SAY

Jerry Schmidt—Evanston, Illinois: "Bill Russell was a winning player. Defense and rebounding are the name of the game, and Russell was the best at both."

Tom Weed—Bozeman, Montana: "He did more for the sport than any other player."

Joe Collins—Denver, Colorado: "The Russell-Chamberlain rivalry was the greatest in sports—and Russell always won."

Marty West—Bethesda, Maryland: "Russell dominated basketball as a player and a coach."

Bill Baldridge—Des Moines, Iowa: "One of the games most intelligent players. He was a leader."

Hughes Norton—Cleveland, Ohio: "...Always a Celtic. He was the epitome of a great center, especially on defense."

The fans chose Bill Russell as their favorite basketball player of all time.

Name in order your three favorite basketball players of all time.

Player	E.	S.	M.	W.	Tot.
B Russell	37	37	43	52	169
W Chamberlain	43	27	41	48	159
B Cousy	37	20	19	39	115
J Havlicek	18	25	20	6	69
J West	7	12	14	29	62
O Robertson	4	9	24	17	54
K Jabbar	5	14	16	6	41
E Baylor	5	3	9	18	35
J Erving	4	6	15	9	34
G Mikan	6	-	20	6	32
B Pettit	-	6	17	-	23
L Bird	6	5	-	5	16
R Barry	3	-	-	10	13
P Arizin	8	3	-	-	11
D Debusshere	6	-	5	-	11
B Bradley	7	-	3	-	10
H Greer	3	2	-	5	10
D Cowens	2	6	-	-	8
B Cunningham	5	2	-	-	7
B Walton	3	-	-	4	7
W Reed	1	5	-	-	6
E Johnson	-	2	-	3	5
J Lucas	-	-	4	1	5
W Frazier	-	1	-	3	4
E Monroe	1	-	3	-	4
W Unseld	-	2	2	-	4
JJ White	2	2	-	-	4
L Costello	-	3	-	-	3
H Gallatin	3	-	-	-	3
E Hayes	-	2	1	-	3
T Heinsohn	1	2	-	-	3
B Howell	-	3	-	-	3
N Johnston	3	-	-	-	3
G King	3	-	-	-	3
B Lanier	-	2	1	-	3

Player	E.	S.	M.	W.	Tot.
C Lovellette	-	3	-	-	3
J Loscutoff	3	-	-	-	3
S Martin	-	-	3	-	3
A Roman	-	3	-	-	3
B Sharman	2	1	-	-	3
R Tomjanovich	-	3	-	-	3
J Twyman	-	-	-	3	3
N Van Leer	-	-	3	-	3
V Barilla	2	-	-	-	2
M Lacourie	-	-	-	2	2
B Leonard	-	-	-	2	2
E McCauley	-	-	2	-	2
C Maxwell	2	-	-	-	2
B Melchione	2	-	-	-	2
R Smith	2	-	-	-	2
V Von Bredakoff	2	-	-	-	2
G Yardley	-	2	-	-	2
N Archibald	-	-	-	1	1
D Bing	-	-	1	-	1
L Dampier	-	1	-	-	1
Flanagan*	1	-	-	-	1
G Goodrich	-	-	-	1	1
C Hagen	-	-	1	-	1
C Hawkins	-	-	1	-	1
L Jackson	1	-	-	-	1
KC Jones	-	-	-	1	1
S Jones	-	-	1	-	1
W Jones	1	-	-	-	1
B Love	-	-	1	-	1
P Maravich	-	-	-	1	1
N Nixon	-	-	1	-	1
C Scott	1	-	-	-	1
W Skoog	-	-	1	-	1
S Tannenbaum	-	1	-	-	1
O Taylor	1	-	-	-	1
B Winters	-	-	1	-	1

*Flanagan (first name unknown), received one third place vote in the East. He played for Little Falls, N.Y., a semi-pro team.

JULIUS ERVING
The Human Side of the Superhuman

"Julius Erving is one of our national treasures," says former NBA Commissioner Larry O'Brien. Irving is even more special in Philadelphia, where he guided the Sixers to the World championship Series in 1976, 1980, and 1982, and finally to a world championship in 1983.

Anyone who has seen "Dr. J" in action understands why he was voted the nation's favorite NBA player. He has a wide repertoire of graceful moves that spellbinds people in arenas across the nation.

"He is a cut above," observed Pat Williams, 76er General Manager. "He's special not only in this country, but all over the world. More importantly, he's a fine human being—humble, unique, gracious, and, if I might add, a fine husband and parent. Everyone looks up to him."

Apparently basketball aficionados across the country also respect Erving. His name was their most frequent response when asked to name their favorite currently active player. Erving's closest rival, Larry Bird, beat him in the East and tied him in the Midwest, but Dr. J's lopsided victories in the South and West gave him first place. Jabbar and "Magic" Johnson also finished with over 100 points.

THE FANS SAY

Joe Collins—Denver, Colorado: "Dr. J can do things the human body can't."

David Turner—Omaha, Nebraska: "Best player to ever play the game. It's actually fun watching him play."

Jerry Schmidt—Evanston, Illinois: "Forward is the toughest position to dominate the game of basketball from, but Julius does it. Unstoppable. A team player."

Ted Lopatkiewitz—Falls Church, Virginia: "I love seeing Erving play. He's flashy yet comes across as a real human being."

Bill Langford—Miami, Florida: "Just super to watch. No one else can make the shots he does. He's magic in motion."

Name in order your three favorite currently active basketball players.

Player	E.	S.	M.	W.	Tot.
J Erving	66	65	66	54	251
L Bird	69	34	66	47	216
K Jabbar	37	35	51	39	162
E Johnson	20	15	32	33	100
M Malone	1	15	3	11	30
G Gervin	4	4	3	10	21
D Dawkins	3	3	4	5	15
Mar. Johnson	3	-	10	1	14
J Sikma	1	-	-	11	12
D Issel	-	3	2	5	11
B Jones	5	5	-	1	11
C Maxwell	3	6	-	-	9
N Nixon	1	-	1	7	9
J Wilkes	-	1	1	6	8
N Archibald	1	2	4	-	7
K McHale	2	-	5	-	7
E Hayes	3	3	-	-	6
I Thomas	1	-	5	-	6
A Toney	-	2	4	-	6
M Kupchak	4	1	-	-	5
D Roundfield	-	5	-	-	5
G Williams	-	-	-	5	5
M Cheeks	1	-	3	-	4
D Johnson	-	-	-	4	4
R Parish	3	1		-	4
D Ainge	-	-	-	3	3
C Ford	1	2	-	-	3
P Ford	-	-	3	-	3
B Lanier	-	2	1	-	3
R Robey	-	3	-	-	3

Player	E.	S.	M.	W.	Tot.
J Vincent	-	3	-	-	3
S Wedman	-	-	-	3	3
M Aguirre	-	-	2	-	2
A Dantley	-	-	-	2	2
L Free	-	-	-	2	2
A Gilmore	-	-	2	-	2
D Griffith	-	2	-	-	2
A King	2	-	-	-	2
B McAdoo	-	2	-	-	2
K Macy	-	1	-	1	2
S Mix	-	-	2	-	2
S Moncrief	-	-	2	-	2
J Moore	-	2	-	-	2
L Shelton	-	-	1	1	2
P Westphal	-	2	-	-	2
B Williams	2	-	-	-	2
F Brown	-	-	-	1	1
J Davis	-	-	1	-	1
K Grevey	-	-	1	-	1
B King	-	1	-	-	1
J Spanarkel	-	1	-	-	1
R Theus	-	-	1	-	1
D Thompson	1	-	-	-	1
K Vanderweigh	-	-	-	1	1
B Winters	-	-	1	-	1

"Julius Erving is one of our national treasures, states former NBA Commissioner Larry O'Brien.

THE DALLAS COWBOYS:
America's Football Team

During the 1970's, the Dallas Cowboys first became known as America's team, and in 1982, the fans picked them as the most popular team in the NFL by a wide margin over the Pittsburgh Steelers. The Cowboys swept the South with 60 points, while also winning the Midwest and the West. The Eagles won the East with 39.

According to Tex Schramm, the Cowboys General Manager, there are many reasons for the popularity of the Cowboys. "People have been brought up with the Cowboys being a winning team. No other team has come close to making the playoffs 16 of the last 17 years like we have."

The Cowboys started as an expansion team in 1962. Despite being underdogs in the early years, they built a strong team through the draft. Tom Landry, the team's only coach has led the team to winning records every year since 1966, five Super Bowls, and two Super bowl victories.

The Cowboys have had more than their share of heroes and exciting games over the past two decades. Football fans will long remember Roger Staubach and the great Cowboy comebacks in the last two minutes of a game; their great defense, led by the likes of Lilly, Howley, Green, Jordan, Waters, White, Renfro, Harris, and Martin; and the explosive runs of Calvin Hill and Tony Dorsett. All these players have helped mold a solid tradition in Dallas.

After the Cowboys and Steelers came the third place Eagles with 81. The state of California filled the next three slots as the 49ers, Raiders, and Rams finished fourth, fifth and sixth. In sectional rivalries, the Cowboys beat the Oilers for bragging rights in Texas. The Steelers over the Eagles for Pennsylvania, the Giants over the Jets for New York City, and the Dolphins beat the Bucanneers for Florida. Near the bottom of the list, the Falcons only received votes in the South, and the Cardinals only tallied a total of eight.

Name your three favorite football teams.

TEAM	EAST	SOUTH	MIDWEST	WEST	TOTAL
Cowboys	23	60	35	37	155
Steelers	35	20	31	19	105
Eagles	39	10	20	12	81
49ers	6	4	15	36	61
Raiders	10	4	12	27	57
Rams	9	8	11	25	53
Giants	31	6	7	—	44
Dolphins	16	16	3	8	43
Bears	1	2	30	9	42
Vikings	1	5	27	7	40
Oilers	3	20	10	5	38
Jets	24	4	6	3	37
Redskins	16	10	8	2	36
Broncos	1	6	1	27	35
Packers	1	6	24	2	33
Bengals	6	6	20	—	32
Browns	5	5	16	6	32
Lions	2	4	22	1	29
Chargers	—	—	9	17	26
Colts	9	10	2	3	24
Patriots	16	4	1	2	23
Seahawks	—	—	3	16	22
Bills	11	3	1	3	18
Falcons	—	18	—	—	18
Chiefs	—	—	9	8	17
Saints	2	12	3	—	17
Bucaneers	2	9	2	—	13
Cardinals	—	—	7	1	8

The Dallas Cowboys were picked by the fans as the most popular team in the NFL.

JIM BROWN
The Fans' Favorite Football Player of All Time

Football's best all time running back, and, in the opinion of many, the game's greatest player, is now its most popular. Jim Brown, with 114 points and strong support in the East, was voted sports fans' favorite football player. John Unitas (84) and Gayle Sayers (75) placed second and third respectively.

"I'd like to thank all the fans who voted for me," Brown said after learning the results. Jim quickly noted, however, that there were many other superstars in his time. "Sam Huff, Big Daddy Lipscomb, Bobby Mitchell, and Timmy Brown were some of the players I admired."

Cleveland's offensive line dedicated themselves to Jim. "They loved me. They always wanted to give me that extra block." Monte Clarke, Mike McCormick, Chuck Noll, Dick Schaftraft, John Hickerson, and John Wooten were among the Cleveland linemen who helped Brown to many NFL records. "Without them I wouldn't have been able to set those records." Brown's records include most yards gained (12,312), most touchdowns (126), most seasons leading the league in rushing (8), and most 100-yard-rushing games (58). However, Brown's greatest thrill in football was not one of his individual accomplishments. "Nothing can match winning the World Championship. We beat Baltimore 27-0 in the 1964 title game."

Jim played for the Browns from 1957-1965. Six years later, in 1971, The Pro Football Hall of Fame officially inducted him into the Canton, Ohio shrine. Today, America's favorite football player lives with his family in Los Angeles, where he is an actor. His latest film, "One Down, Two to Go," was released in November.

THE FANS SAY

Dave Duffy—Villanova, Pennsylvania: "My recollection of Jim Brown was him carrying five Eagles on his back for a large gain time after time."

Tim Hagerman—San Francisco, California: "The first person I identified as a superstar. He's the greatest running back of all time."

Dave Orlinoff—Boston, Massachusetts: "Jim Brown was so much better than everyone else. He stood out from the other players of his time."

James Williams—Little Rock, Arkansas: "When I was a kid growing up, Jim Brown was the best, no one even came close."

Name in order your three favorite football players of all time.

Player	E.	S.	M.	W.	Tot.
J Brown	43	17	31	23	114
J Unitas	10	30	22	22	84
G Sayers	9	14	31	21	75
OJ Simpson	14	10	17	17	58
R Staubach	3	31	8	14	56
J Namath	13	17	8	10	48
B Starr	-	5	18	17	40
D Butkus	4	1	16	12	33
YA Tittle	12	1	10	7	30
S Jurgenson	8	11	5	5	29
J Greene	9	4	6	5	24
P Hornung	7	6	9	2	24
F Tarkenton	3	1	8	11	23
G Blanda	1	17	3	-	21
H McElhenny	-	-	6	14	20
F Gifford	8	2	5	-	15
O Graham	-	9	6	-	15
T Dorsett	4	4	6	-	14
J Taylor	1	6	3	4	15
T Bradshaw	3	2	4	4	13
M Olsen	-	2	2	9	13
L Dawson	-	-	6	5	11
R Nitsche	-	-	8	2	10
L Swann	2	5	1	2	10
C Bednarik	9	-	-	-	9
B Nagurski	3	-	6	-	9
E Campbell	-	6	2	-	8
A Karras	-	3	5	-	8
A Page	-	-	3	5	8
C Trippi	-	8	-	-	8
L Alworth	-	-	-	7	7
R Berry	-	5	-	2	7
C Connerly	3	2	-	2	7
B Dudley	4	-	3	-	7
S Huff	3	-	4	-	7
L Brown	4	-	2	-	6
L Czonka	2	-	1	3	6
S Grogan	6	-	-	-	6
P Warfield	2	2	2	-	6
M Goldberg	5	-	-	-	5
R Grange	3	-	-	2	5
L Groza	-	2	-	3	5
D Meredith	-	4	1	-	5
L Nomellini	-	-	3	2	5
F Ryan	2	-	3	-	5
B Smith	-	-	3	2	5
J Thorpe	5	-	-	-	5
N VanBrocklin	1	-	-	4	5
B Waterfield	-	-	3	2	5

Player	E.	S.	M.	W.	Tot.
S Baugh	-	4	-	-	4
J Brodie	1	-	-	3	4
S Luckman	-	2	-	2	4
W Payton	1	-	3	-	4
P Pihos	2	2	-	-	4
O Taylor	-	-	1	3	4
S VanBuren	4	-	-	-	4
D Walker	-	-	4	-	4
K Anderson	-	-	3	-	3
F Arbanis	-	-	3	-	3
R Bleier	3	-	-	-	3
B Friedman	3	-	-	-	3
C Gilchrist	3	-	-	-	3
F Harris	3	-	-	-	3
J Hart	-	-	3	-	3
E Hirsch	-	-	-	3	3
C Morton	-	-	-	3	3
M Motley	-	-	3	-	3
D Osborne	-	-	3	-	3
K Strong	3	-	-	-	3
R Todd	3	-	-	-	3
B Trumpy	3	-	-	-	3
R Turner	-	-	1	2	3
N Weidlemeir	-	3	-	-	3
E Boozer	2	-	-	-	2
C Conamaker	-	-	2	-	2
BJ Conrad	-	-	2	-	2
T Dean	2	-	-	-	2
M Ditka	-	-	-	2	2
T Fears	-	-	-	2	2
V Ferragamo	-	-	2	-	2
C Green	-	-	-	2	2
B Greise	-	-	-	2	2
J Ham	-	-	-	2	2
T Harmon	2	-	-	-	2
I Harris	-	-	2	-	2
M Hein	2	-	-	-	2
C Hennigan	-	2	-	-	2
B Johnson	-	-	2	-	2
D Jones	1	-	1	-	2
E Jones	-	2	-	-	2
J Kapp	-	-	2	-	2
J Klecko	2	-	-	-	2
J Lujack	-	-	2	-	2
W McDaniels	2	-	-	-	2
A Manning	-	2	-	-	2
H Marshall	-	-	-	2	2
A Parker	2	-	-	-	2
W Paschal	2	-	-	-	2

Name in order your three favorite football players of all time.

Player	E.	S.	M.	W.	Tot.
D Pearson	-	2	-	-	2
L Rentzel	-	2	-	-	2
K Stabler	-	-	2	-	2
J Stallworth	-	2	-	-	2
C Taylor	-	2	-	-	2
J Tyrer	-	-	2	-	2
R White	-	-	-	2	2
L Wilson	-	-	2	-	2
B Agajaniun	-	-	2	-	2
OJ Anderson	-	-	1	-	1
F Bilitnikoff	-	-	-	1	1
D Crow	-	-	1	-	1
I Curtis	-	-	1	-	1
C Foreman	-	-	1	-	1
R Francis	1	-	-	-	1
R Gabriel	-	1	-	-	1
R Gradishar	-	-	-	1	1
T Hill	-	1	-	-	1
C Howley	-	1	-	-	1
C Isbell	-	-	-	1	1
C Joiner	-	-	-	1	1
G Johnson	-	-	-	1	1

Player	E.	S.	M.	W.	Tot.
L Jordan	-	1	-	-	1
B Kilmer	1	-	-	-	1
E Ladd	1	-	-	-	1
B Layne	-	-	1	-	1
B Lilly	1	-	-	-	1
D Little	-	-	-	1	1
B Lurtsema	-	-	1	-	1
T McDonald	1	-	-	-	1
L McQuay	-	1	-	-	1
G Marchetti	-	-	-	1	1
T Mott	1	-	-	-	1
J Orr	-	1	-	-	1
D Pastorini	-	1	-	-	1
J Perry	-	-	-	1	1
J Riggins	1	-	-	-	1
J Robinson	-	-	-	1	1
A Robustelli	-	-	1	-	1
K Rote	-	-	1	-	1
J Schmidt	-	-	1	-	1
J Stenerud	-	-	1	-	1
C Waters	-	1	-	-	1
D White	-	-	-	1	1

Jim Brown was voted the fans' favorite NFL football player of all time.

EARL CAMPBELL
A Hard Working Player

No NFL running back has ever had a better start in his career than Earl Campbell. He led the league in rushing in each of his first three years, and led the AFC in his fourth. The nation's sports fans have acknowledged Earl's great feats, and chosen him as their favorite football player in the NFL today.

There is more to Earl's popularity than his great running ability. "He's a great human being," according to Ed Biles, former coach of the Houston Oilers. "The first thing he did when he came to Houston as a rookie was build a home for his family. The average fan relates to Earl. He's a throwback to the hardnose type of player. He comes to play football and nothing else. You will never see any controversy surrounding Earl."

Earl gathered 32 of his 81 points to lead the South. Recently-retired Terry Bradshaw received 27 votes in the East to lead that region and earn honors as the second most favorite currently-active football player. Tony Dorsett captured third place in the overall voting. In the Midwest, Walter Payton (fourth overall) dominated, while Joe Montana led the voting in the West.

THE FANS SAY

Bill Richard—New Orleans, Louisiana: "He's not a prima donna. Hard-nosed. Always gives 100%."

Sam Bradshaw—Dallas Texas: "Athletically beyond comparison."

John Freidman—Los Angeles, California: "Earl epitomizes the powerful running back but still has finesse."

Name in order your three favorite current football players

Player	E.	S.	M.	W.	Tot.	Player	E.	S.	M.	W.	Tot.
E Campbell	11	32	21	17	81	T Kramer	-	3	16	3	22
T Bradshaw	27	9	20	13	69	J Zorn	-	3	5	14	22
T Dorsett	19	14	24	7	64	K Anderson	2	-	17	-	19
W Payton	4	14	36	9	63	F Harris	5	2	5	7	19
J Montana	2	8	12	26	48	H Carmichael	7	3	3	5	18
D Fouts	3	4	6	24	37	R Jaworski	-	6	7	4	17
D White	3	12	6	14	35	W Montgomery	11	-	2	3	16
B Sims	5	3	16	2	26	R White	3	6	1	5	15
B Sipe	2	6	15	2	25	K Winslow	-	3	2	9	14

Name in order your three favorite current football players.

Player	E.	S.	M.	W.	Tot.
J Hannah	6	7	-	-	13
A Manning	3	7	3	-	13
A Rashad	-	2	5	5	12
K Stabler	-	4	5	3	12
R Todd	5	6	-	-	11
J Delaney	-	-	5	5	10
J Jefferson	1	-	1	8	10
J Lambert	7	-	3	-	10
J Ferguson	6	2	1	-	9
S Grogan	6	2	1	-	9
D Pearson	-	3	2	4	9
R Gradishar	-	-	-	8	8
T Hendricks	3	-	2	3	8
D Pastorini	1	2	3	2	8
D Williams	-	6	2	-	8
S Bartkowski	-	2	4	1	7
D Clark	-	1	-	6	7
C Collingsworth	-	-	5	2	7
V Ferragamo	3	-	4	-	7
G Rogers	1	6	-	-	7
L Taylor	6	-	1	-	7
R Carpenter	6	-	-	-	6
M Gasteneau	6	-	-	-	6
S Largent	-	-	-	6	6
J Plunkett	1	2	-	3	6
W Andrews	-	5	-	-	5
J Bunting	2	-	3	-	5
N Cromwell	2	-	-	3	5
F Dean	-	-	-	5	5
F Lewis	5	-	-	-	5
H Martin	-	2	3	-	5
L Parrish	5	-	-	-	5
J Theisman	5	-	-	-	5
J Klecko	4	-	-	-	4
J Stallworth	2	2	-	-	4
B Chandler	-	3	-	-	3
M Coleman	3	-	-	-	3
R Francis	2	-	1	-	3
S Fuller	-	-	-	3	3
D Hill	-	-	3	-	3
P Johnson	-	-	3	-	3
C Joiner	-	-	2	1	3
B Laird	3	-	-	-	3
J Lofton	-	-	3	-	3
M Malone	-	-	-	3	3

Player	E.	S.	M.	W.	Tot.
A Monk	-	3	-	-	3
C Muncie	-	-	-	3	3
T Myers	-	3	-	-	3
N Olkewicz	3	-	-	-	3
J Riggins	-	3	-	-	3
F Solomon	-	3	-	-	3
P Tilley	-	-	3	-	3
T Couseneau	-	-	2	-	2
J Cribbs	2	-	-	-	2
D Deardorff	-	-	2	-	2
C Dobler	-	-	-	2	2
J Hart	-	-	2	-	2
W Hilgenberg	-	-	2	-	2
K Krepfle	-	-	2	-	2
S Nelson	2	-	-	-	2
J Sciarra	2	-	-	-	2
J Siemon	-	-	2	-	2
J Simpson	-	-	2	-	2
B Van Pelt	2	-	-	-	2
L Wright	-	-	-	2	2
L Alzado	1	-	-	-	1
OJ Anderson	-	-	1	-	1
J Barbara	-	-	1	-	1
W Buchanon	-	-	-	1	1
S DeBerg	-	-	-	1	1
T Franklin	-	-	1	-	1
J Ham	1	-	-	-	1
J Haslett	1	-	-	-	1
T Hill	-	1	-	-	1
E Hipple	-	-	1	-	1
E Jones	-	1	-	-	1
R Lott	-	-	-	1	1
J Miller	-	-	-	1	1
G Neilson	-	1	-	-	1
R Newhouse	1	-	-	-	1
O Newsome	-	1	-	-	1
J Robinson	1	-	-	-	1
R Rucker	-	-	1	-	1
J Sisemore	1	-	-	-	1
J Stenerud	-	-	1	-	1
S Studswell	-	-	1	-	1
M Tatupu	1	-	-	-	1
J Washington	1	-	-	-	1
C White	1	-	-	-	1

THE NEW YORK ISLANDERS
The New Kids in Town

Ten years ago the New York Islanders were the worst team in hockey. They finished the 1972-73 season with twelve wins and six ties in 78 games. But the Islanders were to continue building through the draft, and seven years later they were Stanley Cup Champions, defeating the Flyers four games to two. They repeated as champions in 1980-81, beating the North Stars in six. The Vancouver Canucks fell prey in four straight games in 1982 as the Isles won their third straight Cup. In 1983, the Islanders defeated the Edmonton Oilers, 4-0 for their fourth straight Stanley Cup. The New Yorkers' string of Cup victories was broken by their Edmonton rivals in the fiercely fought 1984 playoffs.

This rags to riches story partially explains the popularity of the Islanders, and their selection as the fans' favorite NHL hockey team. "Our early setbacks followed by the quick turnaround certainly won many fans for us," claims Bill Torrey, General Manager of the Isles. "When you have a winning team, fans are attracted to you. Other reasons for our popularity are the several American-born players that most teams don't have. We're a young team that has grown up together."

The Islanders topped the survey with 129 points, 21 more than the second place Montreal Canadiens. The Bruins, who tied the Isles in the East for first, finished third overall with 89 points. Edmonton placed highest of any former WHA team (7th), while the Maple Leafs (16th) did the worst of any of the six original teams.

Some regions of the country receive little or no hockey coverage:

...A man from Kansas City thought the Scouts were still in the NHL.

...A Sioux City resident chose the Sioux City Muskateers as his third favorite hockey team.

...The Cincinnati Stingers, a defunct WHA club, was one individual's favorite hockey team.

Name your three favorite hockey teams.

NAME	EAST	SOUTH	MIDWEST	WEST	TOTAL
Islanders	42	22	40	25	129
Canadiens	28	15	34	31	108
Bruins	42	11	16	20	89
Flyers	37	11	18	16	82
Rangers	39	15	15	8	77
Black Hawks	2	8	31	16	61
Oilers	10	2	12	16	40
North Stars	3	-	26	4	33
Blues	2	3	20	1	26
Kings	3	-	5	18	26
Capitals	14	11	-	-	25
Sabres	14	2	1	4	21
Penguins	14	5	-	1	20
Canucks	1	1	2	13	16
Red Wings	-	6	10	-	16
Maple Leafs	2	2	5	3	12
Whalers	6	-	-	-	6
Flames	-	4	-	1	5
Scouts	-	-	3	-	3
Stingers	-	-	3	-	3
Rockies	1	-	-	-	1
Muskateers	-	-	1	-	1

The N.Y. Islanders — the fans' favorite NHL hockey team.

GORDIE HOWE

Favorite Hockey Player of All Time

According to Jim Devallano, General Manager of the Detroit Red Wings, "No one ever did it better than Gordie Howe." "He was a legend in Detroit."

"Longevity, I guess. I was there more often," was Gordie Howe's remark upon learning of his selection as hockey's most popular player. Gordie accumulated 151 points, and received strong support in all four sections of the country. Only two other players came close: Bobby Orr with 139 and Bobby Hull with 129 points.

"I put all my effort into every game—like it was my last, and fans remember that." Gordie also added there were certain players that were his personal favorites. "Bobby Orr and Bobby Clarke always excited me with their great hustle and team play." Without realizing it, Gordie described himself, a team player and true hustler.

In 26 seasons, Gordie scored a record 1,850 points and was named a First Team All NHL selection 12 times. Today he is an executive with the Hartford Whalers.

THE FANS SAY

Sam Bradshaw—Dallas, Texas: "Gordie handled himself well on and off ice."

Jeff Hudd—Buffalo, New York: "Gordie Howe was a super hockey player. Not many can be compared to him."

Hughes Norton—Cleveland, Ohio: "I have nothing but the utmost admiration for someone who, at such an advanced age, could still be so great. He's one of the most prolific scorers of all time."

Gordie Howe—the fan's favorite hockey player of all time.

Name in order your three favorite hockey players of all time.

Player	E.	S.	M.	W.	Tot.
G Howe	36	31	47	37	151
B Orr	46	22	32	39	139
B Hull	16	25	45	43	129
P Esposito	26	12	24	5	67
H Richard	24	17	12	11	64
W Gretzky	3	7	7	10	27
B Clarke	15	4	2	2	23
S Mikita	-	-	14	5	19
B Parent	12	3	-	1	16
J Beleveau	2	5	4	-	11
B Geoffrion	2	8	-	-	10
Y Cournoyer	4	-	3	-	7
G Lafleur	6	-	-	-	6
G Chayon	3	-	-	-	3
G Fielder	-	-	-	3	3
G Hall	-	-	3	-	3
T Lindsay	-	2	-	1	3
P Mahoney	-	-	-	3	3
M Marsh	-	-	-	3	3
H Richard	3	-	-	-	3

Player	E.	S.	M.	W.	Tot.
D Sanderson	2	-	1	-	3
T Sawchuck	1	-	2	-	3
R Vachon	-	-	3	-	3
C Conacher	-	-	-	2	2
R Fleming	-	-	-	2	2
E Giacomin	-	-	2	-	2
D Kerr	2	-	-	-	2
N Picard	-	-	2	-	2
B Plager	-	-	2	-	2
E Shack	-	-	-	2	2
G Worsely	-	2	-	-	2
K Dryden	1	-	-	-	1
T Green	1	-	-	-	1
C Johnson	1	-	-	-	1
M Johnson	1	-	-	-	1
A Joliet	-	-	-	1	1
K Magnuson	-	-	-	1	1
J Plante	-	-	-	1	1
D Schultz	1	-	-	-	1
G Unger	-	-	1	-	1
J Watson	-	1.	-	-	1

Fans across the country voted Wayne Gretzky as their favorite current NHL player.

WAYNE GRETZKY

The Fans Favorite
and Record Holder Extraordinaire

Fans across the country voted Wayne Gretzky their favorite current NHL player. After only four years in the league, he was virtually rewritten the record book. A partial list of accomplishments includes his 92 goals in 1982, shattering the old record of 76 goals held by Phil Esposito. Wayne also holds the record for assists (120) and points in a season (212), eclipsing his own mark set the previous year. He also has the distinction of scoring 50 goals the quickest ever in one season, in 39 games—11 games faster than the previous record. Other accomplishments by Gretzky for the 1982 season include one five-goal-game, three four-goal-games, 10 hat tricks and 23 four-point games. In 1983 Wayne scored 196 points as he led the Oilers into the Stanley Cup finals against the Islanders. In 1984, Wayne led the Oilers to the Stanley Cup Championship.

Prior to 1981, no one until Gretzky ever averaged over two points per game. In 1981, he averaged 2.05 points and in 1982 an unheard of 2.65. His career stats after just three years read like the stats of 10 year veterans: 198 goals, 313 assists, and 513 points in 239 games. Wayne Gretzky's name has been engraved in many trophies including the 1980 and 1981 Lady Byng Trophies and the 1980, 1981, and 1982 MVP Awards. For the fans favorite currently active hockey player, Wayne received 257 votes, 187 more than his closest competitor Mike Bossy, which was the largest margin of victory for anyone in any sport in this general category.

Upon learning of the results, Wayne stated, "It is an honor to be considered America's favorite hockey player. However, I honestly feel that it is the result of the team's and the coaches' hard work." Wayne also pointed out that players with good offensive ability get more exposure than others.

The reasons for Gretzky's popularity are numerous. Perhaps the most important is the vast amount of time he donates to charitable organizations. Participating in tennis tournaments, reading public service announcements, and speaking at fund raisers are just some of the activities Wayne is involved in during the summer. There is something special about him that fans across Canada and America adore. As Glen Sather, the Edmonton Oiler coach, pointed out: "Fans flock to the stadiums across the country wherever we play. They all come to see Wayne play."

THE FANS SAY

Tom Weed—Bozeman, Montana: "The new superstar. Gretzky is, without a doubt, the best athlete of the new generation."

Bill Richard—New Orleans, Louisiana: "He's a great competitor and a tremendous athlete."

Dave Orlinoff—Boston, Massachusetts: "I often wonder how he can possibly do all the things he does on the ice. Wayne's rewriting the whole record book."

Name in order your three favorite currently active hockey players.

Player	E.	S.	M.	W.	Tot.
W Gretzky	57	56	70	74	257
M Bossy	27	8	19	16	70
G Lafleur	15	9	6	10	40
B Clarke	17	8	11	3	39
B Trottier	14	4	16	-	34
T Esposito	3	6	15	7	31
M Dione	1	-	-	20	21
B Smith	7	3	10	-	20
C Gillies	10	2	2	4	18
D Potvin	11	2	1	-	14
G Perrault	11	2	-	-	13
D Maruk	3	6	-	3	12
B Park	9	-	-	3	12
B Barber	8	2	1	-	11
B Beck	7	-	2	2	11
B Goring	2	-	-	7	9
W Paiement	-	-	2	7	9
R Carlisle	4	-	-	4	8
C Resch	2	1	2	3	8
R Walters	2	6	-	-	8
B Carpenter	-	7	-	-	7
M Luit	-	-	7	-	7
T O'Reilly	5	2	-	-	7
D Sutter	-	-	2	5	7
R Vachon	-	-	4	3	7

Player	E.	S.	M.	W.	Tot.
D Cicerelli	-	-	6	-	6
I Turnbell	-	-	5	-	5
G Fuhr	-	-	1	3	4
B Plager	-	-	4	-	4
B Propp	4	-	-	-	4
D Savard	-	-	4	-	4
S Christoff	-	-	3	-	3
P Holmgren	3	-	-	-	3
M Lessard	-	-	-	3	3
W Cashman	-	2	-	-	2
J Craig	2	-	-	-	2
B Federko	-	-	2	-	2
M Johnson	2	-	-	-	2
G Meloche	-	-	2	-	2
R Middleton	2	-	-	-	2
B Nichols	-	-	-	2	2
R Ramage	-	-	-	2	2
L Robinson	2	-	-	-	2
G Sargent	-	-	2	-	2
J Tonelli	2	-	-	-	2
W Babych	-	-	1	-	1
M Baron	1	-	-	-	1
N Broten	-	-	1	-	1
M Dion	-	-	1	-	1
R Flockhart	1	-	-	-	1
S Shutt	1	-	-	-	1
D Smith	-	-	-	1	1

THE FANS SPEAK OUT

Should there be a designated hitter in baseball?

	E.	S.	M.	W.	TOT.
Yes	16	19	27	22	84
No	30	25	27	28	110

Chuck Tanner, manager of the Pittsburgh Pirates says: "I've managed in both leagues, and I don't like it because it takes away from late inning strategy."

Phil Rizzuto, Yankee broadcaster: "I like the designated hitter rule. It keeps some of the older players in the game longer. Just think what it would have done for Aaron, Mays, and Mantle."

Pete Rose, Montreal Expo first baseman: "I'm for anything that will add offense to the game—it's just one more bat in the lineup."

Should there be interleague play in baseball?

	E.	S.	M.	W.	TOT.
Yes	23	29	36	23	111
No	24	17	21	21	83

Steve Rogers, Montreal Expo pitcher, feels that the lack of interleague play creates a certain mystique: "No other sport has this structure. Each of the 162 games means more in baseball than any other sport. This makes the World Series the special event that it is."

Pete Rose: "I don't like the idea of interleague play because it would take away from the All Star Game and the World Series."

In all other major sports except football, college athletes can turn pro before their senior year. Should the NFL implement this policy?

	E.	S.	M.	W.	TOT.
Yes	14	23	26	21	84
No	34	20	31	25	110

Ed Biles, former coach of the Houston Oilers: "One of the things that makes the NFL great is the cooperation with colleges.   I think it is important to maintain present regulations so that students can get their degree and graduate."

Do you believe fighting in hockey adds excitement or detracts from the game?

	E.	S.	M.	W.	TOT.
Adds	14	13	19	17	63
Detracts	27	23	31	22	103
No Opinion	6	8	8	6	28

Wayne Gretzky, center for the Edmonton Oilers: "I don't condemn it. There are going to be fights...It is a necessary release of emotion that ultimately prevents more serious acts of violence, such as stick swinging."

A man from St. Louis claims that "fighting is the reason I don't like hockey."

Jim Devallano, General Manager of the Detroit Red Wings: "I personally don't think it adds excitement, but it is part of the game because it is a contact sport."

John McCarthy, Assistant Director of Officiating: "There is a place in hockey for spontaneous fighting, but not for brawling or mass fighting."

Harry Sinden, General Manager of the Boston Bruins: "It is not the actual fighting that adds to the excitement, but the anticipation that excites the crowd and gets them involved. In that sense, it adds a lot."

Do you believe the present playoff structure in hockey is good for the game?

	E.	S.	M.	W.	TOT.
Yes	7	10	15	7	39
No	36	25	33	36	130
No Opinion	2	10	9	4	25

One participant in the survey from Duluth, Minnesota says, "I think the system is terrible," while another from Washington D.C. calls it "goofy."

Harry Sinden: "It's certainly not an ideal system. If you think about it, four of every five teams qualify. I would like to see 12 teams make it."

Gordie Howe: "The NHL is fighting for the fans' interest by keeping more teams in the race longer. In that sense, I feel it is good for the game."

Do you believe the NBA season is too long, too short, of just right?

	E.	S.	M.	W.	TOT.
Long	38	29	42	34	143
Short	1	1	5	—	7
Just Right	8	13	10	13	44

Two basketball fans from Cleveland call the NBA season "a joke" and "pointless."

Red Auerbach, General Manager of the Boston Celtics: "Everyone says it is too long. Several years ago, the owners tried to shorten the season, but the players' union objected because it would have cut players' salaries."

Should video replays be used under certain circumstances to aid officials in professional sports?

	E.	S.	M.	W.	TOT.
Yes	27	25	35	28	115
No	21	18	22	18	79

When asked to respond to the above question, an intoxicated man surveyed in a Kansas City bar replied: "Yes, 10-4, definitely—they're human and make mistakes. The replays would correct them."

A man who only wished to be known as "Dr. X" firmly states, "Yes, they're [the officials] blind as bats."

Red Auerbach: "I don't feel that video replays should be used because of the time factor and they are often inconclusive."

Chuck Tanner: "They shouldn't be used; the decision shouldn't be taken out of the hands of the umpires, whose judgement is generally good."

Another participant from Atlanta makes this suggestion: "I think there should be a qualified official in the press box with access to closed circuit TV to correct bad calls."

Steve Rogers: It might be a good tool, but would probably cause more problems than solutions."

Are professional athletes overpaid, underpaid, or paid just right?

	E.	S.	M.	W.	TOT.
Over	35	34	40	38	147
Under	—	2	2	3	7
Just Right	10	9	15	6	40

If overpaid, in which sport are they the most overpaid?

	E.	S.	M.	W.	TOT.
Basketball	14	17	18	22	71
Baseball	20	13	22	13	68
Football	1	2	4	3	10
Tennis	—	—	—	2	2
Golf	—	—	1	—	1
No Opinion	9	12	10	11	42

Is free agency good or detrimental to sports?

	E.	S.	M.	W.	TOT.
Good	23	30	31	30	114
Detrimental	21	13	22	16	72
No Opinion	1	1	4	2	7

Which sport gives you the most value for your ticket dollar?

	E.	S.	M.	W.	TOT.
Baseball	20	12	29	23	84
Football	12	20	17	12	61
Basketball	5	7	2	1	15
Hockey	5	1	5	4	15
Golf	3	1	3	1	8
Horse Racing	1	—	—	1	2
Soccer	1	—	—	1	2
Track	2	—	—	—	2
No Opinion	—	2	2	1	5

4

THE PLAYERS RATE THE FANS

After rating sports cities on their teams' field performances and the fans' performance at the gate, it seemed that the human element was missing. However, fans can't be surveyed about themselves because they're either too biased or attend games primarily only in their own home town.

The athletes, however, visit almost every city. Who, it might be asked, would be in a better position to evaluate a cross section of the fans than the players? After all, the athletes see every team's fans in their sport. But on what basis can players rate fans? If athletes rate fans on the basis of the climate and scenery in the fans' home base, fans in cities like San Diego would always finish near the top, while those in cities like Buffalo wouldn't appear to have a chance.

The athletes were asked to rate the towns in four areas, three of which relate directly to the fans: the most enthusiastic, the unfriendliest, the most knowledgeable and their favorite city (based upon the quality of the cities accommodations, playing fields, weather, and overall atmosphere).

In the first two surveys (77-78 and 79-80), the players were asked to choose five cities in each category with points awarded on a 5-4-3-2-1 basis (their favorite city could get 5 points etc.). In the 1981-1982 and the 1983-1984 surveys, they were asked to name only three cities. The points awarded were reduced to 5-3-1, hence the lower totals.

Two veteran players from each team in the four major sports were asked to participate in each survey, of which 172 players responded the first two years, while 184 and 185 agreed in the next two surveys. All 98 professional teams had at least one player participate every year.

1977-1978
HOW THE PLAYERS RATE THE FANS
BASEBALL
NATIONAL LEAGUE

Enthusiastic		Unfriendly		Knowledgeable		Favorite Cities	
Philadelphia	83	Philadelphia	59	Chicago	55	San Diego	84
Los Angeles	72	New York	43	Los Angeles	54	Los Angeles	63
Chicago	71	San Francisco	35	Philadelphia	47	Chicago	46
Cincinnati	35	Chicago	33	Cincinnati	38	Philadelphia	46
San Francisco	22	Los Angeles	9	New York	32	San Francisco	30

AMERICAN LEAGUE

Enthusiastic		Unfriendly		Knowledgeable		Favorite Cities	
Boston	81	New York	97	New York	88	Anaheim	48
New York	79	Chicago	38	Boston	82	Boston	46
Chicago	63	Boston	29	Chicago	37	New York	30
Detroit	28	Milwaukee	23	Detroit	31	Chicago	23
Kansas City	23	Cleveland	19	Milwaukee	16	Seattle	21

BASKETBALL

Enthusiastic		Unfriendly		Knowledgeable		Favorite Cities	
Portland	123	San Antonio	48	New York	116	Los Angeles	82
Seattle	109	Philadelphia	44	Boston	73	New York	78
San Antonio	70	New Orleans	30	Portland	54	Phoenix	41
Denver	58	Seattle	29	Philadelphia	53	San Fran/Oak	39
New York	38	Detroit	24	Los Angeles	36	New Orleans	36
Philadelphia	29	Boston	21	Seattle	20	Philadelphia	33
Milwaukee	16	Washington	16	Indiana	15	Seattle	22
Cleveland	16	New Jersey	16	Washington	16	Detroit	20
Boston	13	Phoenix	15	Golden State	15	Denver	18
Washington	9	Cleveland	11	Denver	14	Atlanta	17

FOOTBALL

Enthusiastic		Unfriendly		Knowledgeable		Favorite Cities	
Denver	85	Oakland	65	Dallas	62	San Diego	79
Pittsburgh	44	Philadelphia	61	NY Giants	56	Los Angeles	69
Philadelphia	44	New England	53	Miami	51	San Francisco	62
Miami	40	Baltimore	42	Los Angeles	39	New York	49
New Orleans	40	Denver	36	Green Bay	38	Miami	45
Washington	39	Pittsburgh	36	Pittsburgh	35	New Orleans	37
Green Bay	32	NY Giants	35	Washington	34	Denver	36
New England	32	Cleveland	34	Minnesota	25	Dallas	34
Dallas	31	NY Jets	31	Philadelphia	23	Washington	32
Baltimore	29	Washington	29	NY Jets	19	Oakland	24

HOCKEY

Enthusiastic		Unfriendly		Knowledgeable		Favorite Cities	
Philadelphia	130	Philadelphia	86	Montreal	132	Montreal	75
Boston	66	NY Rangers	75	Toronto	100	Toronto	66
Montreal	54	Detroit	41	Boston	44	Los Angeles	50
NY Islanders	53	NY Islanders	41	Vancouver	37	Vancouver	40
Detroit	33	Boston	34	Detroit	21	Boston	39
NY Rangers	31	Pittsburgh	17	Philadelphia	18	Atlanta	25
Buffalo	30	Toronto	13	Buffalo	15	Denver	19
Toronto	11	Chicago	11	NY Rangers	14	New York	14
Los Angeles	10	Vancouver	11	NY Islanders	7	Chicago	10
St. Louis	9	St. Louis	10	Minnesota	5	Philadelphia	9

Don Stanhouse, pitcher: "The fans in New York are so knowledgeable, they know the first day your baseball card is out."

Lynn Swann, wide receiver: "The fans in Dallas actually look down on you.... They are emotional and abusive in Cleveland. The fans in Pittsburgh, on the other hand, are great—opposing players hate to come here."

Tug McGraw, pitcher: "The Mets' boosters used to be enthusiastic, but not any more. However, I feel the potential is still there ... I love to go to Chicago—it's a great baseball city. It is also a good change of pace, with all day games and early dinners."

Ed Kranepool, first base: "The Met fans are in a dormant stage. They'll come back for a winning team."

Tom Boerwinkle, center: "Fans, in general, are much more knowledge-able and sophisticated about the game. Now they not only appreciate scoring, but also defense, offensive rebounding, and good assists."

O.J. Simpson, running back: "The Los Angeles Ram fan is a sophisti-cated one. He has good knowledge, but is less enthusiastic."

Kurt Ridley, goalie: "The Flyers fans are amazing—they actually have an effect on the opposition. Enthusiasm fills the Spectrum. They're cheering from the moment the Flyers step on the ice for warmups."

Bob Johnson, center: "Steeler fans cheer from the very start. They're more knowledgeable, so they expect more. They are also rougher on the team, and unfriendly."

Mark Fidrych, pitcher: "Yankee fans are the unfriendliest in the country. They are in a class by themselves."

Doug Collins, guard: "I like to go to Phoenix to play only because of the great weather."

Pete Mahovolich, center: "I'm surprised how knowledgeable Flyers fans became in such a short time."

Fran Tarkenton, quarterback: "Fans are not any more sophisticated or knowledgeable than they used to be."

In the 1977-78 survey, the players rated the Chicago Cubs' fans as being the most knowledgeable.

1979-1980
HOW THE PLAYERS RATE THE FANS
BASEBALL
NATIONAL LEAGUE

Enthusiastic		Unfriendly		Knowledgeable		Favorite Cities	
Philadelphia	77	New York	63	Philadelphia	58	San Diego	62
Los Angeles	57	Chicago	59	Los Angeles	49	Chicago	43
Chicago	46	Philadelphia	43	Cincinnati	43	Los Angeles	41
Houston	35	Pittsburgh	24	New York	38	San Francisco	35
Cincinnati	29	San Francisco	15	Chicago	38	Philadelphia	32

AMERICAN LEAGUE

Enthusiastic		Unfriendly		Knowledgeable		Favorite Cities	
New York	99	New York	88	Boston	90	Anaheim	64
Boston	81	Chicago	64	New York	89	Boston	61
Kansas City	48	Detroit	29	Kansas City	42	Kansas City	43
Chicago	43	Boston	26	Baltimore	38	Seattle	37
Baltimore	33	Milwaukee	19	Chicago	22	Dallas/Arlington	37

BASKETBALL

Enthusiastic		Unfriendly		Knowledgeable		Favorite Cities	
Portland	131	San Antonio	92	New York	128	New York	90
San Antonio	88	Boston	57	Boston	82	Los Angeles	88
Seattle	82	Portland	52	Portland	60	San Diego	61
Boston	61	Detroit	50	Philadelphia	54	Seattle	47
Philadelphia	36	Seattle	44	Seattle	40	Houston	35
Milwaukee	28	Phoenix	35	Los Angeles	34	San Fran/Oak	30
Phoenix	21	New York	25	Washington	24	Phoenix	25
New York	19	Philadelphia	23	Milwaukee	22	Portland	23
Atlanta	14	Chicago	22	Chicago	14	San Antonio	23
Denver	13	New Jersey	18	Phoenix	8	Atlanta	22

FOOTBALL

Enthusiastic		Unfriendly		Knowledgeable		Favorite Cities	
Houston	112	Philadelphia	79	Pittsburgh	99	Los Angeles	124
Pittsburgh	101	Oakland	60	Dallas	72	San Diego	109
Philadelphia	97	New England	55	Philadelphia	55	San Francisco	96
Denver	91	Buffalo	53	NY Giants	53	New York	72
Tampa Bay	60	Chicago	50	Houston	51	New Orleans	62
San Diego	46	Denver	48	Green Bay	34	Denver	41
Washington	42	Pittsburgh	44	Los Angeles	34	Oakland	38
Seattle	34	NY Jets	43	Chicago	33	Miami	34
Atlanta	31	Baltimore	40	Washington	28	Philadelphia	28
NY Giants	26	Washington	37	Minnesota	22	Houston	24

HOCKEY

Enthusiastic		Unfriendly		Knowledgeable		Favorite Cities	
Philadelphia	166	Philadelphia	133	Montreal	170	Montreal	124
NY Islanders	77	NY Rangers	132	Toronto	138	Los Angeles	96
NY Rangers	65	Boston	82	Vancouver	53	Vancouver	73
Minnesota	53	NY Islanders	65	Boston	41	Toronto	61
Montreal	49	Chicago	33	Buffalo	40	Boston	59
Buffalo	48	Pittsburgh	22	Philadelphia	27	New York	55
Boston	43	Detroit	15	Quebec	23	Denver	25
Colorado	34	St. Louis	13	Winnipeg	22	Minnesota	25
Chicago	15	Vancouver	13	Edmonton	22	Chicago	19
Detroit	13	Edmonton	11	Minnesota	15	Washington	12

Lyle Alzado, defensive tackle: "I love to visit San Diego in the middle of winter. The 80 degree temperature feels good in the middle of our frigid winters."

Glenn Abbott, pitcher: "The most unruly, loud, and obnoxious fans are in New York City."

Joe Ehrmann, defensive tackle: "The lobster in New England is superb, Seattle is beautiful, but I feel that Baltimore has the nicest people and best fans in the country."

Larry Little, guard: "Football fans are becoming too involved with what is happening on the field. They are too rowdy. They have no right to throw things at players or officials. The only right they do have at a game is to cheer or boo, since they pay."

Roland Office, outfielder: "The 'Bleacher Bums' in Chicago are very unfriendly. They get on most players' nerves.... The fans in Los Angeles are knowledgeable—they acknowledge good plays consistently."

Wally Chambers, defensive end: "I like the cities with stadiums that have grass fields better than those with artificial turf."

Phil Esposito, center: "The fans in Boston are very nice people."

John Fitzgerald, center: "Football fans in the East are different from everyone else. They are blue collar fans and follow their teams to the very end—they live and die with their teams."

Larry Hisle, outfielder: "I like to visit Toronto. It's a clean city where fans come to the park to enjoy the game.... The Yankee fans are most knowledgeable; they always react."

Mark van Eeghan, running back: "There is incredible enthusiasm in Denver and Seattle.... On the other hand, the fans in New England and Pittsburgh are incredibly unfriendly. I never walk off the field after a game without my helmet on.... I love to visit Green Bay—it's like a small, quiet college town."

The Philadelphia Flyers' fans have been rated the most enthusiastic hockey fans in every survey taken since the survey began.

1981-1982
HOW THE PLAYERS RATE THE FANS
BASEBALL
NATIONAL LEAGUE

Enthusiastic		Unfriendly		Knowledgeable		Favorite Cities	
Philadelphia	59	New York	59	Philadelphia	48	San Diego	54
Los Angeles	51	Philadelphia	32	New York	44	Los Angeles	42
Montreal	31	Chicago	28	Cincinnati	38	Chicago	27
Chicago	25	San Francisco	23	Los Angeles	33	New York	12
New York	20	Atlanta	22	Chicago	21	Houston	8

AMERICAN LEAGUE

Enthusiastic		Unfriendly		Knowledgeable		Favorite Cities	
New York	81	Chicago	70	New York	48	Anaheim	51
Chicago	51	New York	57	Boston	44	Boston	41
Boston	46	Detroit	30	Detroit	38	New York	33
Baltimore	20	Oakland	18	Chicago	33	Chicago	23
Oakland	19	Texas	13	Baltimore	21	Oakland	19

BASKETBALL

Enthusiastic		Unfriendly		Knowledgeable		Favorite Cities	
Portland	120	San Antonio	65	New York	124	Los Angeles	70
Boston	61	Detroit	56	Boston	73	New York	61
San Antonio	37	Philadelphia	48	Portland	35	San Diego	48
Seattle	28	Boston	41	Philadelphia	31	Houston	33
Milwaukee	21	New York	27	Los Angeles	26	Phoenix	28
New York	19	Portland	19	Milwaukee	22	Atlanta	21
Los Angeles	17	Utah	15	Washington	19	Seattle	17
Chicago	14	New Jersey	12	Seattle	17	San Fran/Oak	14
Philadelphia	11	Chicago	10	Chicago	14	Philadelphia	12
Phoenix	9	Cleveland	8	Phoenix	12	Boston	11

FOOTBALL

Enthusiastic		Unfriendly		Knowledgeable		Favorite Cities	
Denver	73	Philadelphia	61	Pittsburgh	56	San Diego	98
Philadelphia	71	Buffalo	57	Philadelphia	54	San Francisco	55
Houston	70	New England	50	Dallas	52	New Orleans	50
Pittsburgh	66	Chicago	38	Green Bay	47	Houston	43
Detroit	42	Denver	35	Cleveland	42	Los Angeles	42
Buffalo	38	Cleveland	28	Denver	36	New York	36
Cleveland	28	NY Giants	26	NY Giants	28	Tampa Bay	31
San Diego	26	NY Jets	24	NY Jets	27	Denver	27
Dallas	23	Washington	20	Minnesota	20	Oakland	26
Green Bay	20	Miami	18	Miami	18	Seattle	22

HOCKEY

Enthusiastic		Unfriendly		Knowledgeable		Favorite Cities	
Philadelphia	82	NY Rangers	79	Montreal	135	Los Angeles	96
NY Rangers	52	Philadelphia	75	Toronto	91	Montreal	71
St. Louis	41	Boston	48	Boston	30	Toronto	43
Minnesota	37	Chicago	31	NY Rangers	22	Denver	29
NY Islanders	29	Detroit	26	Quebec	16	Vancouver	22
Quebec	28	NY Islanders	22	Edmonton	11	New York	20
Colorado	21	Quebec	17	Vancouver	9	Minnesota	15
Boston	18	Pittsburgh	14	Minnesota	8	Quebec	12
Montreal	15	Los Angeles	12	Calgary	7	Boston	10
Washington	11	Toronto	8	Buffalo	6	St. Louis	9

Harold Carmichael, wide receiver: "The cities I enjoy going to are the ones where we [the Eagles] have the greatest rivalries, such as Washington and Dallas."

Jerry Koosman, pitcher: "The New York fans are a step ahead of everyone else because of the vast news coverage. Even ten-year-olds buy newspapers to keep up with their favorite teams."

Billy Paultz, center: "The fans in San Antonio are really enthusiastic."

Pete Rose, first base: "They're so knowledgeable in New York because of the newspapers."

Jack McIlhargy, defenseman: "There are two cities I love to visit: Boston because of their aggressive fans, and Montreal because of the great tradition. You can actually feel it when you walk in either building."

Jim Hart, quarterback: "I am becoming more and more disenchanted with fans' behavior. Two incidents stick with me. About five years ago, in Philadelphia, Ron Jaworski was sacked hard and was hurt. The fans there actually started to boo him. I was incensed, so I went over to some of them and gave them a piece of my mind. This is why I picked Eagle fans the unfriendliest.
   The second incident happened just recently, at home in St. Louis. An opposing defensive lineman was injured and our fans started to boo. Dan Deardorff and I stepped out of the huddle to help him off the field and to stop the fans. It sounds like we're going back to the middle ages, doesn't it?"

Ray Burris, pitcher: "Cub fans are enthusiastic regardless of the situation. They generally have good knowledge of the game and applaud excellent performances. The afternoon start adds to the enthusiasm, in my opinion."

Gary Fencik, safety: "Fans in Green Bay appreciate the game more."

Dave "Tiger" Williams, right wing: "All fans are unfriendly to me, and I love it! When fans get on me, I know I got on them. It is evident to me that the American fan is younger than his Canadian counterpart, who is older and more sophisticated. As a result, Americans are more enthusiastic."

1983 - 1984
HOW THE PLAYERS RATE THE FANS
BASEBALL
AMERICAN LEAGUE

Enthusiastic		Unfriendly		Knowledgeable		Favorite Cities	
Chicago	68	New York	70	Boston	52	Anaheim	64
Milwaukee	52	Chicago	46	New York	42	Boston	42
New York	41	Oakland	32	Baltimore	36	Chicago	28
Baltimore	38	Cleveland	24	Detroit	22	Kansas City	22
Boston	24	Detroit	12	Milwaukee	20	Texas	18

NATIONAL LEAGUE

Enthusiastic		Unfriendly		Knowledgeable		Favorite Cities	
Philadelphia	55	New York	58	New York	42	Chicago	53
Atlanta	50	San Francisco	46	Chicago	38	Los Angeles	48
Chicago	36	Chicago	23	Philadelphia	37	San Diego	44
Los Angeles	27	Atlanta	22	St. Louis	34	Atlanta	28
New York	22	Pittsburgh	18	Cincinatti	28	Montreal	25

FOOTBALL

Enthusiastic		Unfriendly		Knowledgeable		Favorite Cities	
Denver	82	Philadelphia	59	New York Giants	54	San Diego	74
Washington	68	New England	55	Dallas	50	San Francisco	65
San Diego	62	NY Jets	51	Pittsburgh	47	Seattle	57
Pittsburgh	58	Pittsburgh	47	Denver	43	New Orleans	51
NY Jets	41	Buffalo	38	Washington	42	Denver	46
Houston	34	Cleveland	31	NY Jets	38	Miami	38
Tampa Bay	30	Atlanta	29	Green Bay	35	Dallas	32
Buffalo	24	NY Giants	24	Miami	33	Green Bay	27
Dallas	22	San Francisco	19	Cleveland	28	Kansas City	25
Philadelphia	19	Denver	17	Chicago	27	New York	21

BASKETBALL

Enthusiastic		Unfriendly		Knowledgeable		Favorite Cities	
Portland	122	San Antonio	74	New York	95	Los Angeles	76
San Antonio	68	New York	52	Boston	88	New York	66
Philadelphia	41	Boston	43	Philadelphia	68	San Diego	44
Boston	28	Cleveland	31	Portland	32	Boston	28
Seattle	19	Philadelphia	29	Milwaukee	23	Atlanta	21
Detroit	17	Detroit	17	Detroit	20	Washington	20
New York	14	Utah	14	Los Angeles	17	Philadelphia	16
Los Angeles	12	Los Angeles	12	Chicago	14	Seattle	15
Chicago	11	Phoenix	8	Seattle	13	Phoenix	10
Phoenix	9	Chicago	7	Dallas	11	Chicago	8

HOCKEY

Enthusiastic		Unfriendly		Knowledgeable		Favorite Cities	
Chicago	71	NY Rangers	71	Montreal	141	Montreal	84
Philadelphia	67	Chicago	64	Toronto	89	Los Angeles	78
NY Rangers	52	Philadelphia	55	Quebec	33	Vancouver	43
Boston	33	Boston	38	NY Rangers	27	Chicago	31
Montreal	28	Pittsburgh	31	Boston	16	New York	22
Vancouver	26	Minnesota	21	Edmonton	12	Quebec	20
Edmonton	22	NY Islanders	17	Chicago	10	Boston	16
Minnesota	19	Toronto	13	Calgary	8	Toronto	12
NY Islanders	14	Winnipeg	11	Minnesota	6	Calgary	11
Quebec	12	Detroit	8	Vancouver	6	Detroit	8

Ken Anderson, quarterback: "Fans are unfriendly in Philadelphia, Oakland, and Cleveland. It's fun if you can turn fans in these cities from cheering for the home team to cheering for us. . . . If I play well in Cincinnati, I get credit; when we lose, I get booed. For quarterbacks, there is never a middle. Fans are that fickle."

Tom McMillan, center: "Trailblazer and Spur fans are the most enthusiastic in basketball. They take the game seriously because they are the only game in town."

5

THE ALL STAR TEAMS OF THE DECADE

BASEBALL

Each year, *The Sporting News* chooses an All Star baseball team (only one team was chosen in the 50's, while American and National League teams were picked thereafter). The player who received the most selections at their position was named to the All Star Team of the Decade.

THE 1950'S—ALL STARS

Position	Years Selected	Player
First Base	3	Ted Kluszewski
Second Base	4	Nellie Fox
Shortstop	4	Ernie Banks
Third Base	3	George Kell
Outfield	5	Stan Musial
Outfield	5	Ted Williams
Outfield	4	Willie Mays
Catcher	5	Yogi Berra
Pitcher (Right)	3	Robin Roberts
Pitcher (Left)	3	Warren Spahn

THE 1960'S—AMERICAN LEAGUE ALL STAR TEAM

Position	Years Selected	Player
First Base	3	Boog Powell
Second Base	6	Bobby Richardson
Shortstop	3	Luis Aparicio
Third Base	7	Brooks Robinson
Outfield	4	Al Kaline
Outfield	3	Tony Oliva
Outfield	3	Carl Yastrzemski
Catcher	3	Bill Freehan*
	3	Elston Howard*
Pitcher (Right)	2	Denny McClain*
	2	Earl Wilson*
Pitcher (Left)	2	Whitey Ford*
	2	Gary Peters*

THE 1960's—NATIONAL LEAGUE ALL STAR TEAM

Position	Years Selected	Player
First Base	3	Orlando Cepeda*
	3	Willie McCovey*
Second Base	3	Bill Mazeroski
Shortstop	3	Maury Wills
Third Base	4	Ken Boyer*
	4	Ron Santo*
Outfield	7	Willie Mays
Outfield	4	Hank Aaron
Outfield	4	Roberto Clemente
Catcher	3	Joe Torre
Pitcher (Right)	4	Juan Marichal
Pitcher (Left)	4	Sandy Koufax

*Tie

Willie Mays was named an All Star in seven different seasons during the 1960's.

THE 1970's—AMERICAN LEAGUE ALL STAR TEAM

Position	Years Selected	Player
First Base	2	Dick Allen*
	2	Rod Carew*
	2	John Mayberry*
Second Base	4	Rod Carew
Shortstop	2	Luis Aparicio
	2	Bert Campanaris
Third Base	3	Greg Nettles
Outfield	4	Jim Rice
Outfield	3	Reggie Jackson*
	3	Fred Lynn*
Outfield	3	Bobby Murcer*
	3	Joe Rudi*
Catcher	4	Thurman Munson
Pitcher (Right)	5	Jim Palmer
Pitcher (Left)	2	Frank Tanana

THE 1970's—NATIONAL LEAGUE ALL STAR TEAM

Position	Years Selected	Player
First Base	4	Steve Garvey
Second Base	5	Joe Morgan
Shortstop	2	Larry Bowa*
	2	Dave Concepcion*
	2	Gary Templeton*
Third Base	4	Mike Schmidt
Outfield	3	Cesar Cedeno
Outfield	3	George Foster
Outfield	3	Dave Parker
Catcher	5	Johnny Bench
Pitcher (Right)	2	Ferguson Jenkins*
	2	Tom Seaver*
Pitcher (Left)	4	Steve Carlton

*Tie

BASKETBALL

Since 1947, first and second NBA All Star teams have been chosen by writers and broadcasters. In order to select a team for each decade, two points were given to a player for each year he was a First Team choice, and one point for each time he appeared on the Second Team. The points were then tallied for each decade, and the players chosen.

THE 1950's—FIRST TEAM ALL STARS

Position	Points	Player
Forward	16	Dolph Schayes
Forward	10	Bob Petit
Guard	16	Bob Cousy
Guard	10	Bill Sharman
Center	10	George Mikan

THE 1950's—SECOND TEAM ALL STARS

Position	Points	Player
Forward	7	Paul Arizin
Forward	7	Ed Macauley
Guard	7	Bob Davies
Guard	5	Slater Martin
Center	9	Neil Johnston

THE 1960's—FIRST TEAM ALL STARS

Position	Points	Player
Forward	18	Elgin Baylor
Forward	11	Bob Petit
Guard	18	Oscar Robertson
Guard	14	Jerry West
Center	16	Wilt Chamberlain

THE 1960's—SECOND TEAM ALL STARS

Position	Points	Player
Forward	8	Jerry Lucas
Forward	4	Rick Barry
Guard	7	Hal Greer
Guard	6	Bob Cousy
Center	11	Bill Russell

Dolph Schayes was the leading point getter for All Star honors in the 1950's.

THE 1970's—FIRST TEAM ALL STARS

Position	Points	Player
Forward	11	John Havlicek
Forward	9	Elvin Hayes
Guard	10	Walt Frazier
Guard	8	Jerry West
Center	15	Kareem Abdul-Jabbar

THE 1970's—SECOND TEAM ALL STARS

Position	Points	Player
Forward	7	Rick Barry
Forward	6	Spencer Haywood
Guard	7	Tiny Archibald
Guard	6	Pete Maravich
Center	3	Dave Cowens

Several times during the 70's, John Havlicek made the All Star team as a forward for the Boston Celtics.

FOOTBALL

U.P.I. and A.P. annually selects NFL Offensive and Defensive All Star Teams. One point was awarded for a player named by one of the two news services. If both U.P.I. and A.P. agreed on a player for a position, two points were awarded. The points were tallied, and the Team of the Decades chosen.

THE 1950's—ALL STAR TEAM
OFFENSE

Position	Number of selections	Player
End	5	Harlan Hill
End	5	Pete Pihos
Tackle	9	Lou Groza
Tackle	8	Rosey Brown
Guard	8	Dick Stanfel
Guard	5	Louis Creekmur*
	5	Duane Putnum*
Center	6	Frank Gatski
Quarterback	9	Otto Graham
Halfback	8	Ollie Matson
Halfback	7	Frank Gifford
Fullback	6	Jim Brown

DEFENSE

Position	Number of selections	Player
Defensive End	8	Len Ford
Defensive End	7	Andy Robustelli
Tackle	7	Leo Nomellini
Tackle	7	Art Donovan
Guard	6	Les Bingaman
Linebacker	10	Joe Schmidt
Linebacker	9	Chuck Bednarik
Linebacker	6	Bill George
Defensive Back	11	Jack Christiansen
Defensive Back	7	Robert Dillon
Defensive Back	7	Emlen Tunnel

Otto Graham was an All Star quarterback for the Cleveland Browns in the 1950's.

THE 1960's—ALL STAR TEAM
OFFENSE

Position	Number of selections	Player
End	6	Del Shofner
End	5	Mike Ditka
Tackle	14	Forrest Gregg
Tackle	9	Jim Parker
Guard	9	Jerry Kramer
Guard	6	Gene Hickerson
Center	11	Mick Tingelhoff
Quarterback	6	Johnny Unitas
Running Back	10	Jim Brown
Running Back	10	Gayle Sayers
Running Back	6	Lenny Moore

DEFENSE

Position	Number of selections	Player
Defensive End	10	Deacon Jones
Defensive End	9	Willie Jones
Tackle	11	Bob Lilly
Tackle	9	Henry Jordon
Linebacker	7	Bill Forester
Linebacker	6	Dick Butkis
Linebacker	6	Chuck Howley
Defensive Back	8	Herb Adderly
Defensive Back	7	Bobby Boyd
Safety	9	Willie Wood
Safety	8	Larry Wilson

Deacon Jones—the Rams All-Pro defensive end and a member of the 1960's All Star Team.

THE 1970's—ALL STAR TEAM
OFFENSE

Position	Number of selections	Player
Tight End	8	Dave Casper
Wide Receiver	6	Cliff Branch*
	6	Harold Jackson*
Wide Receiver	6	Lynn Swann*
	6	Gene Washington*
Tackle	14	Ron Yary
Tackle	11	Art Shell
Guard	12	Larry Little
Guard	12	Tom Mack
Center	9	Jim Langer
Quarterback	4	Bob Greise*
	4	Roger Staubach*
	4	Fran Tarkenton*
Running Back	10	O.J. Simpson
Running Back	7	Walter Payton
Kicker	4	Jim Bakken

DEFENSE

Position	Number of selections	Player
Defensive End	12	Jack Youngblood
Defensive End	10	Claude Humphrey
Defensive Tackle	15	Joe Greene
Defensive Tackle	13	Alan Page
Linebacker	14	Jack Ham
Linebacker	10	Bill Bergey
Linebacker	9	Chris Hamburger*
	9	Willie Lanier*
Cornerback	11	Roger Wehrli
Cornerback	7	Willie Brown*
	7	Michael Haynes*
Safety	11	Ken Houston
Safety	9	Paul Krause*
	9	Jake Scott*
Punter	8	Ray Guy

*Tie

Willie Brown — perhaps the greatest defensive halfback to ever play professional footall — was inducted into Pro Football's Hall of Fame on July 28, 1984.

HOCKEY

Voting for the NHL All Star teams is conducted by representatives of the Professional Hockey Writers Association. In order to select a team for each decade, two points were awarded to a player for each year he was a First Team All Star, and one point for each time he appeared on the second team. The points were tallied and the Team of the Decades chosen.

THE 1950'S—FIRST ALL STAR TEAM

Position	Points	Player
Goalie	8	Jaques Plante
Defense	12	Doug Harvey
Defense	12	Red Kelly
Center	10	Jean Beliveau
Right Wing	15	Gordie Howe
Left Wing	12	Ted Lindsay

THE 1950'S—SECOND ALL STAR TEAM

Position	Points	Player
Goalie	7	Terry Sawchuk
Defense	9	Bill Gadsby
Defense	3	Tom Johnson
Center	4	Henri Richard
Right Wing	10	Maurice Richard
Left Wing	4	Dickie Moore*
	4	Sid Smith*

THE 1960'S—FIRST ALL STAR TEAM

Position	Points	Player
Goalie	13	Glenn Hall
Defense	13	Pierre Pilote
Defense	8	Tim Horton
Center	13	Stan Mikita
Right Wing	15	Gordie Howe
Left Wing	17	Bobby Hull

THE 1960'S—SECOND ALL STAR TEAM

Position	Points	Player
Goalie	4	Ed Giacomin
Defense	6	Doug Harvey
Defense	5	Jaques Laperriere*
	5	Bobby Orr*
Center	8	Jean Beliveau
Right Wing	4	Ken Wharrem
Left Wing	9	Frank Mahovlich

THE 1970'S—FIRST ALL STAR TEAM

Position	Points	Player
Goalie	11	Ken Dryden
Defense	10	Bobby Orr
Defense	10	Brad Park
Center	11	Phil Esposito
Right Wing	10	Guy Lafleur
Left Wing	6	Richard Martin

THE 1970'S—SECOND ALL STAR TEAM

Position	Points	Player
Goalie	6	Tony Esposito
Defense	9	Denis Potvin
Defense	6	Borje Salming
Center	6	Bobby Clarke
Right Wing	4	Ken Hodge
Left Wing	5	Bobby Hull

*Tie

Juan Samuel is projected as the National League's All Star second baseman in 1989.

6

THE 1989 ALL STARS

Most fans know that anything can happen in sports, especially in five years. So, in an attempt to foresee the future, a multi-organizational pro sports poll was conducted to project All Star teams for the year 1988. While these projections may not be as precise as I would like them to be, it will be interesting to see how many of the athletes named will be playing in their sports in the 1989 All Star games. It should be noted that all ages mentioned in this chapter are 1989 ages.

In basketball, football and hockey, one or two excellent draft picks could turn a franchise around. This is usually not true in baseball. Normally, it takes years for a player to develop. Since many of baseball's future stars are in major league farm systems, the experts polled in baseball were asked which teams they felt would be in the playoffs in 1989. The consensus:

National League East: The New York Mets would have a slight edge in a close battle involving all six teams.

National League West: The Dodgers are loaded with young talent, but the Padres and Braves are not far behind.

American League East: The Tigers have the youngest talent with the Orioles a close second.

American League West: Seattle's pitching should carry them to the western crown. The Royals should give them a run down the stretch.

IN THE WORLD SERIES, the Tigers will edge the Dodgers four games to three. Maybe!!!

NATIONAL LEAGUE PROJECTED
1989 FIRST ALL STAR TEAM

POSITION	PLAYER	AGE IN 1969	COMMENTS
Catcher	Tony Pena	31	Excellent receiver; hit .301 with 15 homers in 1983
First Base	Gerald Perry	27	Top fielder and has speed; hit .314 with 13 homers at Richmond in 1983
Second Base	Juan Samuel	27	Hit .330 with 15 homers in 65 games at Portland in 1983
Third Base	Pedro Guerrero	29	Hit .298 with 32 homers and 103 RBI's in 1983
Shortstop	Shawon Dunston	25	First overall pick in 1982 draft; great arm; hit .310 at Quad Cities in 1983.
Outfield	Darryl Strawberry	26	Rookie of the year in 1983; hit 26 home runs.
Outfield	Kevin McReynolds	29	Hit .377 with 32 homers and 116 RBI's at Las Vegas in 1983.
Outfield	Brad Komminsk	28	Can do it all; hit .334 with 24 homers and 26 stolen bases at Richmond
Pitcher (left)	Sid Fernandez	26	13-4 with 209 K's in 153 innings at San Antonio in '83.
Pitcher (right)	Mark Grant	26	Was 10-8 with 159 K's at Shreveport; great fastball.

Dwight Gooden has the potential to be a "super" star.

NATIONAL LEAGUE NOTES

CATCHER

Tony Pena should be the Number 1 All Star for years. Gary Carter (35) and Terry Kennedy (32) may be at other positions. Gil Reyes, Robbie Wine (27), Darren Daulton (26) and John Gibbons (26) are potential All Stars.

FIRST BASE

Three stars in the 1983 Dodger organization are potential All Stars at first base—Greg Brock, Mike Marshall and Sid Bream. All three have excellent power. Perry appears to be the best all round players at this position. Francisco Melendez (24) is great defensively and has power.

SECOND BASE

Samuel will be the class of the league at second. Tim Raines (28) may move back to second base. Johnny Ray and Rich Renteria are also solid. Ryne Sandberg could blossom into the best in the league.

THIRD BASE

Nick Esasky (29) and Tim Wallach (30) are power hitters, but not in the class of Guerrero. Chris James (26) has excellent power.

SHORTSTOP

Dunston will be the best all-round shortstop. Ozzie Smith (32) and Gary Templeton (33) will still be excellent fielders.

OUTFIELD

Unlike other positions, there are many young outfielders who could be All Stars in 1989. Other than the six listed above, Herm Winningham (26) and David Green (28) look the best. Other names to remember: Joe Carter (29), Candy Maldonado (28), Andy Van Slyke (28), Trench Davis (28), and Von Hayes (29). Andre Dawson and "Bull" Durham are established stars who will still be producing in 1989. Jeff Stone (26) might be the next Lou Brock. The Gwynn brothers will hit for average.

PITCHER

The four pitchers projected to be All Stars in 1989 all have great fastballs. Fernando Valenzuela (28) should still be a 20-game winner. Other big winners in 1989 might be Ron Robinson (27), Charlie Hudson (26), Jose Deleon (28), Jimmy Jones (25), Craig McMurtry (29) and Ron Darling (28).

In 1989, Fernando Valenzuela will only be 28.

AMERICAN LEAGUE PROJECTED
1989 FIRST ALL STAR TEAM

POSITION	PLAYER	AGE IN 1989	COMMENTS
Catcher	Lance Parrish	32	Hit 27 HR's and drove in 114 runs in 1983 with Tigers.
First Base	Kent Hrbek	28	Hit .297 with 16 homers in 1983 with Twins.
Second Base	Tim Teufel	29	Hit .323 with 27 homers with Toledo in 1983.
Third Base	Brook Jacoby	28	Hit .315 with 25 HR's for Richmond in 1983.
Shortstop	Cal Ripkin Jr.	28	MVP in the American League in 1983.
Outfield	John Morris	27	MVP in Southern Assoc. in 1983. hit 23 homers at Jacksonville.
Outfield	Harold Baines	30	Hit .280 with 20 homers in 1983 with White Sox.
Outfield	Tom Brunansky	28	Hit 20 homers in 1982 rookie season and 28 in 1983 with Twins.
Pitcher (left)	Juan Nieves	24	Great prospect; 6-1 with 0.70 ERA at Beloit.
Pitcher (right)	Jose Rijo	24	Florida St. MVP. won 15 games with 1.68 ERA at Fort Lauderdale in 1983.

Kent Hrbek has the potential to be a superstar.

Robin Yount has been a great shortstop for several years but may be shifted to third base.

AMERICAN LEAGUE NOTES

CATCHER

Skinner is one of many catching prospects. Others are Don Slaught (29), Jeff Reed (25) and Jerry Willard (28).

FIRST BASE

Jim Wilson (Buffalo) is the most feared hitter, but hasn't developed consistency. Orestes Destrada (26) has returned from an injury and should be a great power hitter. Mark McGuire (6'5", 215 lbs.) could be the next Dave Kingman. Mike Rubel (6'4", 215 lbs. and Alvin Davis are future power hitters.

SECOND BASE

Harold Reynolds (27) and Lou Whitaker (31) are excellent fielders. Whitaker hit .320 in 1983. Damasco Garcia (32) will be a veteran.

SHORTSTOP

The American League is loaded with shortstop talent. Ripkin and Yount are two of baseball's best players. Other future stars are Fernandez, Dick Schofield (26), Darnell Coles (26), Bobby Meacham (26) and Curtis Wilkerson. Jeff Kunkel, son of umpire Bill Kunkel, could be great.

THIRD BASE

Weak position. Randy Ready (29) hit .329 at Vancouver. Howard Johnson and Donall Nixon (26) are possibles.

OUTFIELD

Not as strong as the National League. Kurt Gibson (31), once hailed as the next Mickey Mantle, has the potential. Other possible All Stars are Nelson Simmons (26), Daryl Boston (26), Mike Young (28) and Don Mattingly (28).

PITCHER

Storm Davis (27), Dan Petry (30) and Mike Moore (29) will be seasoned veterans by 1989. Other young players to watch are Mark Gubicza (26), Bill Wegman (25), Tim Birtsas (26) and Gene Nelson (28), Mike Boddicker (28), Bruce Hurst (28) and Bud Black (27).

The Houston Rockets projected Akeem Olajuwon as a future star when they made the former University of Houston star the #1 pick in the 1984 draft. The rights to Olajuwon, who opted for the NBA draft as a junior in college, were won in a coin flip by the Rockets over the Portland Trail Blazers.

NATIONAL BASKETBALL ASSOCIATION
PROJECTED 1989 ALL STARS
FIRST TEAM

POSITION	PLAYER	AGE IN 1989	HEIGHT	COLLEGE
Center	Ralph Sampson	28	7'4"	Virginia
Forward	Larry Bird	31	6'9"	Indiana State
Forward	Keith Lee	26	6'11"	Memphis St.
Guard	Ervin Johnson	29	6'9"	Michigan St.
Guard	Michael Jordan	25	6'4"	North Carolina

SECOND TEAM

POSITION	PLAYER	AGE IN 1989	HEIGHT	COLLEGE
Center	Patrick Ewing	26	7'0"	Georgetown
Forward	Terry Cummings	28	6'10"	DePaul
Forward	James Worthy	29	6'9"	North Carolina
Guard	Andrew Toney	30	6'3"	S.W. Louisiana
Guard	Isiah Thomas	27	6'1"	Indiana

NBA NOTES
CENTER

Three centers should be superstars in the late 80's—Sampson, Ewing and Akeem Olajuwon (Houston '85). Other potential stars are Sam Bowie (Kentucky '84), Benoit Benjamin (7'0", Creighton '86) and Chris Washburn (6'11", 1988).

FORWARDS

There are many forwards who could be All Stars in 1989. The above four will be challenged by Dominique Wilkins (Atlanta), Wayman Tisdale (Oklahoma '86), Billy Thompson (Louisville '86), and Sam Perkins (North Carolina '84). Kevin McHale, Adrien Dantley, and Mark Aguirre are current stars. Danny Manning (Kansas '88) will be a great one.

GUARDS

Jordan will be a dominant player in the NBA. Other possible All Stars are Jeff Malone (Mississippi St. '83), Quinton Dailey (Bulls '82 first pick), Darrell Griffith, Maurice Cheeks, Sidney Moncrief and Reggie Theus.

Pat Ewing will be one of the dominant centers of the 1980's.

PROFESSIONAL FOOTBALL
PROJECTED 1989 ALL STARS
FIRST TEAM OFFENSE

POSITION	PLAYER	AGE IN 1989	HEIGHT	WEIGHT	COLLEGE
Wide Receiver	Willie Gault	28	6'2"	190	Tennessee
Wide Receiver	Mark Duper	27	5'10"	183	S.W. Louisiana
Tight End	Tony Hunter	28	6'4"	234	Notre Dame
Tackle	John Ault	26	6'7"	275	Iowa
Tackle	Bill Fralic	26	6'6"	285	Pitt
Guard	Sean Farrell	28	6'2"	260	Penn State
Guard	Mike Munchak	28	6'2"	262	Penn State
Center	Mike Baab	29	6'4"	270	Texas
Quarterback	Dan Marino	28	6'4"	228	Pitt
Running Back	Eric Dickerson	28	6'3"	215	SMU
Fullback	Keith Byars	24	6'2"	235	Ohio St.
Punter	Reggie Roby	28	6'3"	210	Iowa

SECOND TEAM OFFENSE

POSITION	PLAYER	AGE IN 1989	HEIGHT	WEIGHT	COLLEGE
Wide Receiver	Mike Quick	28	6'3"	190	N. Carolina
Wide Receiver	Irv Fryar	27	6'0"	195	Nebraska
Tight	Kellen Winslow	31	6'5"	242	Missouri
Tackle	Dean Steinkuler	26	6'4"	270	Nebraska
Tackle	Anthony Munoz	30	6'6"	278	USC
Guard	Brad Budde	31	6'4"	264	USC
Guard	Dave Dressler	27	6'3"	245	N. Carolina
Center	Steve Mott	28	6'2"	255	Alabama
Quarterback	John Elway	28	6'4"	210	Stanford
Running Back	Curt Warner	27	6'1"	210	Penn St.
Fullback	James Jones	28	6'2"	225	Florida
Punter	Rohn Stark	30	6'3"	195	Florida St.

OFFENSIVE NOTES

WIDE RECEIVERS

Anthony Carter and Trumaine Johnson are the best in the USFL. Other outstanding receivers will be Dennis McKinnon, Jerry Butler, Hassan Jones (Florida St. '86) and Kenny Jackson.

TIGHT ENDS

Kellen Winslow will be 31 in 1989. If he avoids injuries, he will still be an All Star. Todd Christensen and Blair Bush are other potential All Stars. Gordon Hudson (BYU '84) is the best young tight end.

TACKLES

Fralic (Pitt '85) should be the best. Mark Adickes (6'5"-285) and John Fitzpatrick (6'8"-260, USC '86) have great potential. Harvey Salem, Luis Sharpe and Bubba Paris are young starters in the NFL now. Brian Blados (6'6"-300) and Guy McIntyre are other potentials.

GUARDS

All four guards listed above are close in talent. Bruce Matthews can play both guard and tackle as can Steinkuler. Brad Edelman (6'6"-260) is also Pro Bowl material. Doug Dawson and Terry Long could develop.

CENTERS

Baab is clearly the best now. Dave Rimington may wind up being the best. Tom Dixon (Michigan '84) and Tony Slaton are other possibles.

QUARTERBACKS

It takes time to develop an NFL quarterback, so this is a tough position to project. Marino did not take much time; however, Elway with more protection could still be the best. Steve Young (BYU '84), Dave Wilson and Tony Eason are young quarterbacks with a bright future.

RUNNING BACK

Herschel Walker will be a star in the USFL or NFL. Dickerson's rookie year puts him at the top. Other great runners should be Gerald Riggs, Marcus Allen, Mike Rozier, Walter Abercrombie and Robert Weathers.

FULL BACK

Keith Byars (Ohio St. '86) should be the best. James Jones and Roger Craig (6'1"-217) are close behind.

Denver's John Elway, shown during his days at Stanford, is thought by many scouts to have the best potential of any quarterback prospect in more than a decade.

FIRST TEAM DEFENSE

POSITION	PLAYER	AGE IN 1989	HEIGHT	WEIGHT	COLLEGE
Defensive End	Ricky Bryan	27	6'5"	270	Oklahoma
Defensive End	Mike Pitts	29	6'5"	260	Alabama
Defensive Tackle	Leo Wisniewski	28	6'2"	260	Penn St.
Defensive Tackle	John Cannon	29	6'4"	255	William & Mary
Linebacker	Lawrence Taylor	30	6'3"	237	N. Carolina
Linebacker	Hugh Green	29	6'2"	225	Pitt
Linebacker	Vernon Maxwell	28	6'2"	225	Arizona St.
Cornerback	Ronnie Lott	30	6'0"	199	USC
Cornerback	Egypt Allen	25	6'2"	180	TCU
Safety	Ken Easley	30	6'3"	206	UCLA
Safety	Dennis Smith	24	6'3"	212	USC

SECOND TEAM DEFENSE

POSITION	PLAYER	AGE IN 1989	HEIGHT	WEIGHT	COLLEGE
Defensive End	Mike Cofer	28	6'4"	270	Alabama
Defensive End	Keith Willis	27	6'1"	255	Northeastern
Defensive Tackle	Fred Smerlas	32	6'3"	270	Boston College
Defensive Tackle	T.J. Turner	26	6'4"	250	Houston
Linebacker	Mike Merryweather	27	6'2"	212	U. of Pacific
Linebacker	Billy Ray Smith	28	6'4"	230	Arkansas
Linebacker	Ricky Hunley	26	6'2"	230	Arizona
Cornerback	Mike Richardson	28	6'3"	206	Arizona St.
Cornerback	Roynell Young	30	6'1"	186	Alcorn St.
Safety	Terry Kenard	28	6'1"	190	Clemson
Safety	Dwight Hicks	33	6'1"	189	Michigan

DEFENSIVE NOTES

DEFENSIVE END

Mark Gastineau (6'5-276) should still be a factor. Jeff Bryant (29) and Mike Bell (31) should still be solid. Reggie White and William Fuller have potential.

DEFENSIVE TACKLE
Andrew Provence (29) and Lester Williams (27) could develop into Pro Bowl players. Tim Marshall (Notre Dame, 6'4"-250) and Michael Carter could develop. William Perry (6'3"-320) is also a possibility.

LINEBACKERS
Lawrence Taylor will still be the best. Wilbur Marshall (Florida '84), Jack Del Rio (USC, 6'4"-239), and Ron Rivera could be great pro linebackers.

CORNERBACK
Everson Walls will still be an interception leader. Roy Horton and Leonard Smith may develop. Mossy Cade (Texas '84) and Russell Carter (SMU '84) should be starters.

SAFETY
Dennis Thurmond and Bobby Kemp are solid safeties. Joey Browner, Terry Hoage and Tommy Wilcox could be future all pros. Jerry Gray (Texas '85) is young, but should be ready.

Lawrence Taylor, the N.Y. Giants' superstar linebacker, will continue to be a dominant force in the NFL for several years.

NATIONAL HOCKEY LEAGUE
PROJECTED 1989 FIRST ALL STAR TEAM

POSITION	PLAYER	AGE IN 1989	COMMENTS
Goalie	Roland Melanson	28	2.66 goals against average for Islanders in 1983.
Defense	Ray Bourque	27	Best young defenseman in hockey; scored 73 points in '83.
Defense	Paul Coffey	27	Great on the power play; scored 96 points in '83.
Right Wing	Brian Bellows	25	Scored 65 points in rookie season.
Left Wing	Glenn Anderson	27	Scored 104 points in '83.
Center	Wayne Gretzky	28	Hockey's greatest talent; has led league in scoring for 4 years.

NATIONAL HOCKEY LEAGUE
PROJECTED 1989 SECOND ALL STAR TEAM

POSITION	PLAYER	AGE IN 1989	COMMENTS
Goalie	Pete Peeters	31	NHL's top goalie in 1983; 40-11-9 record with 2.36 GAA.
Defense	Phil Housley	25	Excellent point man; scored 66 points in 1983.
Defense	Brian Lawton	24	First American to be #1 pick in draft.
Right Wing	Mike Bossy	32	Scored 118 points in '83.
Left Wing	Mark Messier	28	Scored 106 points in '83.
Center	Mario Lemieux	23	Best player in Junior Hockey in '84; has great potential.

Bryan Trottier, mainstay of the N.Y. Islanders, is a quality player.

NHL NOTES

GOALIE

There are many good young goalies in the NHL. Kelly Hrudey, Tom Barrasso, Andy Moog, Grant Fuhr and Pelle Lindburgh could be top flight goalies in 1989.

DEFENSE

Gordon Kluzak and Gary Nylund were picked as 1988 All Stars. Other good defensemen will be Dave Christian, James Patrick, Mark Johnson, Charlie Huddy and Ken Morrow.

WINGS

Other possible All Stars at wing are Ron Sutter, Bobby Carpenter, Paul Cyr, Steve Larmer and Dennis Maruk.

CENTER

Although Gretzky dominates this position, there are other good young centers in the NHL. Dennis Savard and Bryan Trottier are proven stars. Ron Francis heads a list of others which includes Dale Hawerchuk, Barry Pederson, Neal Broten and Danny Daoust. Pat LaFontaine could also be a future star.

7

CHILDHOOD SPORTS HEROES

Almost every kid has a sports hero. On every sandlot, in every playground, in every schoolyard, in every corner of the country, there are dozens of miniature Pete Roses, Babe Ruths, Wayne Gretzkys, Olga Korbuts and Jim Browns. Some of these dreamers grow up to be somebody else's hero, and some grow up to be stockbrokers and died-in-the-wool fans.

Whatever else happens, the thrills, the hard work, the dreams and the memories live on. Not only do the fans still worship their favorite heroes, so do current and former players. The magic still enchants.

A lot of kids now consider John Elway as their sports hero. John had his own hero in Roger Staubach. Roger had several heroes — Otto Graham and Johnny Unitas amongst them. His all-time favorite personality was Cincinnati Reds' slugger Ted Kluszewski. So it goes.

Part of the enjoyment of putting together this survey book lay in talking to sports stars and celebrities. I chuckled at Andy Rooney's wit, listened to an excited David Steinberg describe Bob Cousy's ball-handling heroics, and loved every second of Gabe Kaplan's remembrances of Duke Snider and Ebbets Field in Brooklyn. I sat in Carroll O'Connor's dressing room after a play as he and his wife shared their thoughts about Babe Ruth and other heroes of their childhood days.

I was thrilled to find that Gordie Howe, Roger Staubach, Robin Roberts and Yogi Berra—some of the stars of my own youth—would pause to share their heroes with me. In this chapter, they and many others will also share them with you.

WILLIAM PROXMIRE
WISCONSIN

United States Senate

WASHINGTON, D.C. 20510

August 19, 1983

Mr. Robert A. McMahon
Borough of Media
P.O. Box "A"
Media, Pennsylvania 19063

Dear Bob:

I am told you wanted to know who was my favorite boyhood sports idol and why. The answer, of course, is that I had a whole bunch of them and here are four.

One was Hack Wilson who was the fabulous Chicago Cub and who still has the record - I think 56 homeruns in a single season in the National League and the all time record anywhere for runs driven in, which was a fantastic 190. Hack was short and stubby and had some personal problems but he could write symphonies that would last through the ages with that baseball bat.

Second was Chris Cagle, who was a running back with Army in the mid-20's. I saw Cagle when Army and Navy tied 21-21 at Soldiers Field in Chicago in about 1927. Cagle was marvelous and when I was a little boy of 11 or 12, I was smitten for life.

Then, of course, there was Red Grange who has that fabulous opening day of his career against Michigan around about 1924-1925 in which he went for a touchdown the first five times he touched the ball and richly earned that great moniker of "The Galloping Ghost".

There was a fourth athlete who played at the University of Chicago, of all places in the 20's. He was captain and center on their team around about 1925 or 1926 when Amos Alonzo Stagg was coaching. Stagg let me sit on the bench with the players and go into the locker room with Ken Rouse. Wow - what a day! Rouse was a superb blocker, great defensive player and a fine gentleman, especially to a little 10 year old kid.

Thanks for the inquiry and once again thanks for your super book.

Sincerely,

William Proxmire, U.S.S.

Chris Cagle — Army's star running back in the mid-20's — is one of Senator William Proxmire's boyhood sports idols.

SPORTS PERSONALITIES
Current Stars

Fernando Valanzuela, Pitcher L.A. Dodgers: Roberto Clemente, "I never saw him play, but I admired him. I heard a lot of great things about him."

Steve Sax, Second Base L.A. Dodgers: Willie Mays, "He was the best there was."

Greg Brock, First Base L.A. Dodgers: Harmon Killebrew, "He was a home run hitter, and that's what I wanted to be."

Mike Sciossia, Catcher L.A. Dodgers: Johnny Bench, "I was a catcher as a kid and Johnny Bench was the best ever at the position."

Steve Garvey, First Base San Diego Padres: Gil Hodges, "He reminded me of my father who was also a first baseman. I was lucky to be able to travel with the Dodgers as a youngster when they were at spring training. Gil used to play catch with me."

Von Hayes, Outfielder Philadelphia Phillies: Ted Williams, "I loved the Red Sox. We are both left-handed hitters, but that's where the similarity ends."

Jim Rice, 1983 A.L. Home Run Champ: Hank Aaron, "I didn't have one as a child, but as I grew up I admired Hank Aaron."

Carl Yastrzemski, Future Hall of Famer: San Musial, "He was the greatest hitter in the game."

Wade Boggs, A.L. Batting Champ: Reggie Jackson, "He was THE home run hitter. I used to imitate him in stick ball games as a kid."

Juan Samuel, Second Base Philadelphia Phillies: Cesar Cedeno, "I really looked up to him because he played hard. I want to play that hard."

Julio Franco, Shortstop Cleveland Indians: Garry Templeton.

Robin Yount, All Star Shortstop: Willie Mays, Willie McCovey, Orlando Cepeda, "I lived in L.A. but the Giants were always my favorite team."

Cecil Cooper, All Star First Baseman: None, "The first major league game I ever saw, including TV, was when I played my first game for the Red Sox."

John Elway, Quarterback Denver Broncos: Roger Staubach: "He was always a great competitor and a winner. I liked the way he maintained his composure under pressure."

Dave Righetti, No-hit Pitcher New York Yankees: Willie McCovey, "I was a big Giants fan when I was a kid. Willie was a great home run hitter."

Dale Murphy, All Star Atlanta Braves: Willie Mays, "I grew up in the Bay area. Willie was the best ever."

Isiah Thomas, All Star Detroit Pistons: Muhammed Ali

Reggie Theus, NBA All Star: Jerry West and Wilt Chamberlain.

Reggie Jackson, Future Hall of Famer: Duke Snider

Rod Carew, Future Hall of Famer: Hank Aaron, "It was fun following the old Milwaukee Braves — Aaron, Logan, Torre, etc."

Joe Cribbs, All Star Running Back: Johnny Rodgers of Nebraska

Dennis Potvin, All Star New York Islanders: Jean Belliveau, "He was the biggest star where I grew up."

Bryan Trottier, All Star New York Islanders: Jean Belliveau, "Like most kids, my heroes changed every year. Belliveau was usually one of the them."

Alan Trammell, All Star Shortstop: Willie Mays, "He could do it all."

Lance Parrish, All Star Catcher: Roberto Clemente, "He was The Best."

Keith Hernandez, All Star First Baseman: Stan Musial, "I always wanted to be a first baseman. Everything Stan Musial did was great. I just wanted to emulate him."

Darrell Strawberry, 1983 Rookie of the Year: Dave Parker, "To me he was the complete player. He played my position. I wanted to be like him when and if I got to the pros.

Tom Seaver, Future Hall of Famer: "Sandy Koufax, He was the ultimate pitcher. Sometimes I would wish I was left-handed to be more like him."

Dale Berra, Shortstop Pirates: Tim and Larry Berra, my older brothers, "Tim Played for the Baltimore Colts."

Dave Parker, All Star Outfielder: Jim Brown, "I always wore #32 as a kid. The Browns were my favorite team, and he was the premier running back."

Dave Concepcion, All Star Shortstop: "When I was a kid and had a bat in my hand, I was Rocky Colavito. Rocky played winter ball in my country (Venezuela) when he was young. He could really hit the ball a long way. When he hit four homers in one game in the American League, it was a big event in Venezuela."

Mike Schmidt, Major League Home Run King: Jim Brown, "I painted #32 on my football helmet when I was a kid, so I could copy Jimmy Brown."

Pete Rose, "Charlie Hustle": Johnny Temple, "I was a Reds fan and Temple played my position. When I came up with the Reds, he was my roommate."

Tug McGraw, Pitcher Philadelphia Phillies: Hank McGraw, "My brother was the best hitter I ever saw."

Mark Howe, All Star Philadelphia Flyers: Gordie Howe, "After every game, he would patiently answer all my questions about hockey."

Julius Erving, America's favorite basketball star: Elgin Baylor, "I admired him for his great play and Bill Russell for his style."

Wayne Gretzy, Edmonton Oilers Superstar: Gordie Howe, "He was my only hero; he was the best."

Former Stars

Robin Roberts, Baseball Hall of Famer: Lou Gehrig and Bill "Swish" Nicholson", "I always admired both, but I was lucky enough to play with Bill late in his career (1950)."

Cookie Rojas, Retired Infielder: Nellie Fox, "He was small like me, and he accomplished a lot for his size."

Yogi Berra, Hall of Famer: Joe "Ducky" Medwick, "I was a Cardinal fan as a youngster, and Joe was my favorite."

Richie Ashburn, Two Time N.L. Batting Champ: Ike Kinnan, semi-pro Ballplayer, "We didn't know any major leaguers in Nebraska. This was the best player I saw as a kid."

Roger Staubach, Former Cowboys Great: Ted Kluzewski, "He was something else. Ted was an awesome power hitter. . . . Otto Graham was my favorite football player. He was the best quarterback I ever saw."

Gordie Howe, Former Hockey Great: Abe Walsh, "I asked him for an autograph after his hockey game. He took me in the club house, had everyone autograph my book and gave me a hockey stick. I'll never forget that. It was my biggest thrill."

Stan Musial, Baseball Hall of Famer: Paul Waner and Carl Hubbell, "I always wanted to hit like Paul Waner and pitch like Carl Hubbell.

Ted Williams — the childhood sports idol of many individuals — felt that Charles Lindbergh was his real boyhood hero.

Ralph Kiner, Hall of Famer: Babe Ruth, "When I was growing up, The Babe was everything."

Bill Bradley, U.S. Senator, Former NBA All-Star: Stan Musial, "He always seemed to come through in the clutch and he was modest."

Ted Williams, Baseball's last .400 hitter: Charles Lindbergh, "He was my real hero—the epitomy of adventure. Babe Ruth and Roger Hornsby were my favorite ball players when I was young."

Managers

Tommy Lasorda, L.A. Dodgers: Joe DiMaggio, "Because he was the greatest Italian player I ever saw."

Chuck Tanner, Pirates: Mel Ott, "We were both left-handed. I wanted to hit like him."

Sparky Anderson, Detroit Tigers: Bob Feller, "He was from Iowa, and I was from South Dakota."

Broadcasters

Earl Weaver, ABC Broadcaster: The Gas House Gang, "I liked the whole Gas House Gang in St. Louis—Marty Marion, Pepper Martin, Leo Durocher and Ducky Medwick."

Al Michaels, ABC Broadcaster: Duke Snider, "I grew up near Ebbets Field in Brooklyn. Duke had everything—power, speed—and was a great clutch hitter."

Harry Kalas, Voice of Notre Dame: Camilio Pascual, "He pitched the first game I ever saw. He was a great pticher on a bad ball club."

Brent Musberger, CBS Sports Broadcaster: Stan Musial, "He always carried himself well."

Referees

Jake O'Donnell, NBA Ref: Tom Gola, "I saw every home game he played at La Salle. I used to pay 50 cents a ticket just to get in to see him play."

Celebrities

David Steinberg, Comedian: Bob Cousy, "I liked short flashy players who hustled. I loved watching Cousy play."

Steve Landesberg, Actor (Barney Miller): Joe DiMaggio, "My biggest thrill was meeting with Joe DiMaggio at Old-timers Day at Yankee Stadium in 1983. Mel Allen signalled me to come over to see him."

Ed McMahon, Actor (Tonight Show): Jim Thorpe, "There was a man who excelled at EVERYTHING."

Julius Erving's boyhood sports idol was Elgin Baylor — the former Laker great.

Gary Burghoff, Actor (MASH): Mickey Mantle and Yogi Berra, "I loved the great Yankee teams between 1953 and 1956."

Andy Rooney, Journalist, Newscaster: "I had many. Among them were Chris Cagle, Eleanor Holme, Jesse Owens, Glen Cunningham and Adolph Keefer. The greatest athlete I ever saw was Frank Gifford. I even named my bulldog after him."

Dan Rather, CBS New Anchorman: Bobby Jones, Halfback for John Reagan High School in Houston. "Best broken field runner I had ever seen. He never quit." Bill Dickey, "Because my late father admired him and because he was the working man's player. He showed up every day and gave you all he had." Joe Louis, "He was a great sport. He ALWAYS had something good to say about his opponent."

Steve Lawrence, Entertainer: Joe DiMaggio, "I loved him. Recently, I got to know him and have dinner with him. What a thrill!"

Edyie Gorme, Entertainer: Sandy Koufax

Bob Hope, Entertainer: Tris Speaker, "I just admired him; he was such a good ballplayer.

Carroll O'Connor, Actor: "I had many. Babe Ruth—he was baseball. Glen Cunningham—he ran the fastest mile of his day. Ace Parker—a great triple threat man with the old Brooklyn Dodgers football team. Others were Jesse Owens, Archie Moore and Gregory Rice."

Gabe Kaplan, Entertainer: Duke Snider, "I used to stand in a gas station on Bedford Avenue across from Ebbets Field and wait for the Duke to hit one in batting practice."

Robert Goulet, Entertainer: Ted Williams, "I was born in Lawrence, Mass., so the Red Sox were my team and Ted was my hero."

Bill Kurtis, CBS News Broadcaster: Bob Matthias, "He was the best all-round athlete."

ACKNOWLEDGMENTS

No one writes a book alone.

I greatefully acknowledge the help of the league offices, the public relations departments of the various clubs and the players who participated in the surveys.

Special thanks are extended to Steve D'Avanzo, Bonnie Dean, and Sue McSherry for the organizational help, and to Jay Searcy and Bill Lyon of *The Philadelphia Inquirer* and Bob Creamer of *Sports Illustrated* for having the confidence in my surveys to put them into print. I also owe particular gratitude to Alan Simpson of the *All-American Baseball News,* Pete Silverman of the New York Rangers, Pat Williams of the Philadelphia 76ers, and Gary Horton of the Tampa Bay Bucs.

A final thank you goes to the 194 people who graciously participated in our national survey. Without them, this book would have been impossible to complete.

THE AUTHOR

Bob McMahon is a 41-year old stock broker in Philadelphia, Pennsylvania. Over the past three years, he has presented over 200 investment seminars in Pennsylvania, New Jersey, and Delaware. A former college economics teacher, he released his first set of sports surveys in 1975 during his first year of teaching. Mr. McMahon served as an infantry lieutenant in Viet Nam. He won the Bronze Star and two air medals.